Norwegian Emigration
Between Rocks
and
Hard Places

Norwegian Emigration
Between Rocks
and
Hard Places

By
Ann Urness Gesme

ISBN: 978-0-578-90388-0

Anundsen Publishing Company
Decorah, Iowa

DEDICATION

IN LOVING MEMORY OF MY HUSBAND OF 70 YEARS

DEAN HARTLEY GESME, SR.
DECEMBER 31, 1928 - OCTOBER 9, 2020

AND

IN HONOR OF MY CHILDREN AND MY CHILDREN'S CHILDREN,
AND IN RECOGNITION OF THE
HERITAGE THAT ILLUMINATES OUR LIVES.

CONTENTS

ACKNOWLEDGEMENTS

The joy, circumstances, and purpose of publishing this book are truly unique. Initially, the idea was to simply reprint the original book. At the encouragement and involvement of my three children Dean Jr., Karen, and Martha, we worked together applying our various skills in business, writing, travel, publishing, as well as a mutual appreciation for our heritage. The result is an expanded version now titled *Norwegian Emigration: Between Rocks and Hard Places.*

This book is dedicated to my husband, Dean Hartley Gesme, Sr., who died October 9, 2020, just as we started this project. Through our 70 years of marriage, we shared the ideals of our heritage and passed them on to our children, grandchildren, great-grandchildren, and others. We both valued and played supportive and leadership roles in organizations to further these ideals.

It has been a most gratifying experience to enlist the experience of my three children to republish this book as I turn 93. It has been a pleasure to spend countless hours with my children on ZOOM and conference calls as we went through each chapter to discuss all aspects of publishing this book. Over the course of the past year, we went through each chapter, considered hundreds of pictures and images, and clarified specific points. We selected new content from my research, writing, and presentations accumulated since the first printing in 1993.

We were fortunate for the historical resources of Vesterheim Norwegian-American Museum and the expertise of Laurann Gilbertson, Vesterheim's Chief Curator, and Jennifer Kovarik. They helped us identify artifacts in the museum that amplify the content of this new book. Norske Folkemuseum is the source for a number of photos from the late 19th Century. Other illustrations are from books published in the early 1800s before photography. My thanks to Ingebjørg Njøs Storvik, manager of the Urnes Stav church, for giving us permission to use personal photographs taken during numerous visits to the Urnes Stav Church. Other photographs came from daughters Karen and Martha, nephew Jon Urness, niece, Edith Urness Pondillo, and Gregory Rohlfing. Photos of carvings that I commissioned are attributed in the captions to the artisans who made them. Additional thanks to Edith and my son, Dean Jr. for proofreading. My thanks also go to Anundsen Publishing in Decorah, Iowa, and to Erik Anundsen for his capable assistance.

PREFACE

*B*etween *Rocks and Hard Places* was published in 1993 and is now out of print. Rather than simply reprinting the original book, and considering the modern conveniences of communications and technology, it has been a joy to work with my three children who offered their sincere interest and many talents to produce this updated version titled *Norwegian Emigration: Between Rocks and Hard Places*. The text of the original book is preserved in its entirety along with new content drawn from the past three decades of continuous research, writing, and presentations since the original book.

Over 75 years ago an assignment for my first-year Norwegian class at St. Olaf College sparked an initial search for information. It was 1945. I was 17 years old, and many of my great aunts and uncles (who seemed extremely old at that time), as well as both of my grandmothers, were still living. I picked their collective brains to gather enough information to fulfill my class requirement, and for the time being, let it go at that. I am eternally grateful to my Norwegian instructor, Esther Gulbrandson, who required her students of Norwegian background to study more than just the language of Norway. It was her aspiration for kindling curiosity about our ethnic backgrounds that stimulated the first spark of interest in writing about my ethnic origin.

After college, I taught in Emmons, Minnesota where I met my future husband, Dean. He was also of Norwegian heritage. We were married the following summer. My interests in genealogy expanded to include both of our families.

Thus began an intense yearning for information about our forefathers. The result is the four books in the *Look to the Rock* series;

Between Rocks and Hard Places; and now, *Norwegian Emigration: Between Rocks and Hard Places.*

> *Look to the Rock... the Gesme Episode, 1985*
>
> *Look to the Rock... the Urness/Barsness Episode, 1988*
>
> *Look to the Rock... the Dybdahl/Anderson Episode, 1991*
>
> **Between Rocks and Hard Places, 1993**
>
> *Look to the Rock....the Talle Episode, 2005*
>
> **Norwegian Emigration: Between Rocks and Hard Places, 2021**

The word "rock" is common to all my books. This was inspired by my Norwegian history college professor, Karen Larson, whose first lecture began with Isaiah 51: 1 (KJV)

> *"Hearken to me, all ye that seek the Lord: look to the rock from which ye are hewn and the whole of the pit from whence ye were digged."*

Books, written in the English language by British and Americans who traveled in Norway during the 1800s, offered a treasure trove of information. These travelers were not the average tourists we think of today but were most often men (very few women) who were interested in fishing, mountaineering, or just sightseeing in out-of-the-way places. Norway was considered by foreigners to be a novel place to visit, a very primitive and exotic country inhabited by an eccentric and primitive population. These intrepid individuals usually traveled in style with a retinue of servants and found lodging with the local minister or government official. They often considered themselves of a higher social status than the Norwegian farmers and peasants. Such local dignitaries helped to reinforce the prejudiced view of Norway's peasantry held by many travelers. Some travelers misinterpreted what they observed of Norwegian folk customs and lifestyle, and left rather incredible accounts while others were more objective. Many left well-written accounts and credible interpretations of social conditions as they existed at that time. Another valuable source of information, written in the Norwegian language, is the local histories (*Bygdebøker*) published in Norway.

Ninety percent of all Norwegians that came to America arrived after the Civil War ended in 1865, however, most of my husband's and my emigrant ancestors left Norway before the Civil War began. The first of our ancestors immigrated in 1843, and the last one in 1880. Those who emigrated before 1860 left Norway as family units as was customary at that time. Those who left Norway as unmarried young adults traveled in the company of one or more of their siblings.

Perhaps the greatest difference in the experiences of the first of our ancestors to leave Norway and the last was in the emigrant journey. The majority of our ancestors came by sailing ship to America. Those who came before 1854 landed in New York, and those who came between 1854 and the end of the 1860s landed in Quebec, Canada. Only the last ones to immigrate experienced the luxury of traveling by steamship.

Through years of research and many trips to Norway, I came to know my forefathers, not as deceased ancestors, but as real live people who were once young and vigorous. *Norwegian Emigration: Between Rocks and Hard Places* is not meant to be a complete account of all Norwegian emigrants. It is an account of our Norwegian immigrant ancestors' living conditions in their home districts of Norway, the circumstances that led to their emigration, their journey, and their new home in America.

> *It is vital in all cultural life to maintain a link between the present and the past. If there is anything that history makes clear it is this, that when a people becomes interested in its past life, seeks to acquire knowledge in order to better understand itself, it always experiences an awakening of new life.*
>
> —*Ole Edvart Rolvaag*

Chapter 1

NORWAY

Norway is a constitutional monarchy situated in the northernmost part of West Europe and currently has a population of just over 5.4 million people. It borders the western edge of the Scandinavian Peninsula and faces the Atlantic Ocean and the North Sea. The word Norway (*Noreg* or *Norge*) means the "way to the north."

As the crow flies, Norway measures about 1,100 miles from north to south; but due to the country's many fjords and islands, she has a coastline of about 12,500 miles. The widest part of the country is 270 miles across, and at the narrowest, it is only 4 miles across. The total land area of Norway is about equal to the size of the state of New Mexico. Norway shares a border of almost 1000 miles with Sweden, 400 miles with Finland, and just over 100 miles with Russia.

One-third of the country lies above the Arctic Circle, making Norway appear to be a polar country; however, the warmth of the Gulf Stream gives it a much more temperate climate than would be expected. During winter Norway's ports are ice-free. The northernmost point of Norway lies as far north as Point Barrow, Alaska, while the latitude at the southernmost point is comparable to that of Juneau, Alaska.

A complete geographical report of Norway was published by the Naval Intelligence Division of the Admiralty in Great Britain during World War II. According to that report, the extremes in temperature in the inner fjord regions were a maximum of 77 degrees F. and a minimum of 4 degrees F. The eastern interior had a maximum of 82 degrees F. and a minimum of minus 30 degrees F. In winter there was snow cover for 45 days in the inner fjord region, and for 150 days in the eastern interior. The fjord regions had an abundance of rain and fog, and in the eastern interior rainfall was described as "adequate." Sogn and Oppland, where most of my ancestors lived, had about 7.5 hours of daylight (including twilight) in winter, and 22.5 hours of daylight in summer; while North Norway had 24 hours of daylight in summer, and 24 hours of dark in winter. Over 70% of the country is made up of lakes, glaciers, mountains, and wasteland, while 24% is covered by forests. Less than 4% of the land is tillable and suitable for cultivation.

Travel brochures refer to five large regions in Norway; *Sørlandet* (South Norway), *Østlandet* (East Norway including the area around Oslo fjord), *Nord Norge* (North Norway), *Vestlandet* (West Norway), and *Trøndelag* (Mid-Norway).

Over hundreds of years, county boundaries have been redefined, reorganized, and renamed. As cities grew and the population shifted in the districts, some areas were reorganized. From the beginning of Danish rule in 1387, and through the years of Swedish rule (1814-1905), Danish terms were used to identify Norway's districts. Following her independence Norwegian terms soon replaced Danish terms. What was once called the *amt* (the Danish word for county), became the *fylke* (Norwegian word for county). For example, Sogn was once a part of *Nordre Bergenhus Amt*; but after 1905 it became a part of the new county, *Sogn or Fjordane Fylke*.

The most recent change was January 1, 2020, when Norway reduced the number of counties from 18 to 11. **Nordland, Rogaland, Møre og Romsdal**, and the city of **Oslo** still have the same borders and names as before, but the rest of the country has been organized into 7 counties with new names and boundaries:

> **Agder**: formerly Aust Agder and Vest Agdger
> **Viken**: formerly Buskerud, Akershus and Østfold
> **Troms og Finnmark**: formerly Finnmark and Troms
> **Vestland**: formerly Hordaland and Sogn og Fjordane
> **Trøndelag**: formerly Nord-Trøndelag and Sør-Trøndelag
> **Innlandet**: formerly Oppland and Hedmark
> **Vestfold og Telemark**: formerly Telemark og Vestfold

Counties and Municipal Counties in Norway

Up until 1918 amt	1918 to 2020 fylke	As of 2020 flyke
Akerhus	Akershus	Viken
Bratsberg	Telemark	Vestfold og Telemark
Buskerud	Buskerud	Viken
Finnmarken	Finnmark	Troms og Finnmark
Hedemarken	Hedmark	Innlandet
Jarslberg	Vestfold	Vestfold og Telemark
Kristians	Oppland	Innlandet
Lyster og Mondal	Vest-Agder	Agder
Nordre Bergenhus	Sogn og Fjordane	Vestland
Nordre Trondhjem	Nord Trøndlag	Trøndelag
Nedenes	Aust-Agder	Agder
Nordland	Nordland	Nordland
Romsdal	Møre og Romsdal	Møre og Romsdal
Søndre Bergenhus	Hordaland	Vestland
Søndre Trondhjem	Sør Trøndelag	Trøndelag
Smaalenens	Østfold	Viken
Stavanger	Rogaland	Rogaland
Tromsø	Troms	Troms og Finnmark
Municipal Counties		
Christiania	Oslo	Oslo
Bergen	Bergen	Bergen

Fylker (counties) are further divided into areas called herred (township) and kommune (city, town, village).

The Lutheran Church became the state church of Norway in 1537. Church divisions included bispedømme or stift (diocese), and further divisions to the prestegjeld, sogn or sokn (parish), and menighet (congregation). It remained the State Church of Norway until 2012.

Counties in Norway as of 2020

A Mini-history of Norway

During the Ice Age (about 25,000 years ago) an enormous glacier moved across the part of Europe which is now Norway, carving out Norway's rugged mountains and deep fjords. As temperatures rose the immense sheet of ice melted, and the country became habitable. Migrants from the German tribes to the south wandered into Norway and established settlements along the coast. Before long, thriving communities were established. By the fifth and sixth centuries, descendants of these tribes had developed a rich and flourishing civilization. Women tended the flocks and provided for the preparation and storing of food, while the men sought iron ore, hunted, and fished. The close proximity of the settled areas of Norway to the sea made seafaring a natural occupation.

At first, Norway was made up of a number of small kingdoms, each ruled by its own chieftain or jarl. Among these rulers of the north were the Vikings who led expeditions to Iceland, Greenland, Ireland, England, Russia, and Europe. Not only were they responsible for plundering, raiding, and robbing, but they also established settlements and carried on trade while exercising significant political and economic influence in their area of contact.

Two of the most important events in the early history of Norway took place at this time: 1) the country was united into one kingdom, 2) paganism was replaced with Christianity. It was around AD 872 that Harald the Fairhair succeeded in uniting Norway for the first time.

The first efforts at introducing Christianity in Norway were made by Harald's son, Haakon the Good, but when Haakon met with opposition by the heathens he chose to join them rather than oppose them. It was Olav Tryggvason, one of Norway's most important early kings, who at last succeeded in converting some areas of Norway to Christianity by both noble and violent means (mostly the latter) beginning in the year 995. Still, the people of Norway were very slow in accepting the new religion.

Olav II Haraldsson was the ruler of Norway from 1016 to 1028. His reign ended in conflict when his countrymen turned against him and pledged their loyalty to the Danish king who they thought would give them more freedom in religious and other matters. In 1028 Olav was forced to flee to Russia. Later he returned to Norway and was attempting to re-establish himself as ruler over a unified and Christian Norway when he met his death in the Battle of Stiklestad in 1030. Soon after his death, Norway accepted the new religion, and Olav was subsequently declared a saint.

While efforts were being made to Christianize Norway, Eirik the Red and his son, Leif Eiriksson, were establishing the first settlement of Europeans on the North American continent in about the year 1000, and called it "Vinland." A few years later, an Icelander, Torfinn Karlsefni, led an expedition of 60 men and 5 women to establish a colony there. Torfinn was married to Gurid, Eirik the Red's widowed daughter-in-law from Greenland. Their son, Snorre Torfinnson, born about 1010, is said to be the first white child born in America. When the natives in Vinland became hostile, the colonists left the settlement and returned to Greenland after only three years in North America.

Woodcut of Viking Ship by Hans Gerhard Sørensen, 1980
Vesterheim Norwegian-American Museum, Decorah, IA

Following Leif Eiriksson's expedition to "Vinland" in North America, the Vikings became firmly established in Ireland and England. The Norman Conquest of 1066 spelled the end of most raids by Norsemen. The Viking Age came to a close, and with its demise, raiding and plundering by the feared Scandinavians stopped. Instead of planning Viking expeditions to other countries, the people of the North now concentrated on bringing some semblance of order to their own country. A system of rules and regulations was developed which provided a means of protection for a person and his property. However, no means of law enforcement was provided. To compound the problem, any and all of the kings' sons, including illegitimate sons, could become rulers. At this time in history, it appears that kings' sons were an unruly lot with an extraordinary appetite for power. Under such conditions, it was impossible to settle differences in a peaceable manner. As a result, chaos reigned among the people of Norway for over a century.

King Magnus the Law-Mender (Lagabøte), who ruled for seventeen years in the latter half of the 13th century was so named for his being the first to collect the old laws and form the common law for all of Norway. Under his leadership, the country became a better organized state than most other countries in Europe. His rule brought relative peace, and thus transient stability prevailed in Norway, but it was unfortunately short-lived. Soon after his death in 1280, discord returned. At first, it was between the church and state, and later within the church itself.

The 14th century brought disaster to Norway. The Medieval Culture was beginning to disintegrate and Norway found herself organizationally exhausted, lacking the vigor needed to replace the old culture with something new. The Renaissance was gaining impetus in Europe, but there was virtually no evidence of such a revival in this remote part of the world. Signs of decline were already apparent when in 1349, a ship from England came into the harbor at Bergen, bringing with it the bubonic plague or Black Death, as it was called. Of the less than one-half million people in Norway at the time, over one-third died of the disease. In the more densely populated areas, as well as among the clergy and officials who had contact with large numbers of people, the toll was heaviest. Later epidemics in 1359 and 1371 reduced the population even more so that the population, in general, was reduced by one-half, and the clergy and nobility by four-fifths. All construction of churches ceased, farms were left deserted, and the country was in a state of utter desolation. According to some historians, some areas were completely depopulated. It took Norway more than three centuries to repopulate the deserted areas and to regain the level of population she had prior to the plague in 1349.

When the Black Death swept through Norway, it was especially devastating in some areas, including Hedalen in Valdres. Few people living there survived, and those who did live moved to other districts less severely hit by the disease. Farms were deserted and became overgrown with trees and brush. Buildings tumbled down, becoming totally obliterated after many decades. Eventually, even the little Hedal church was entirely swallowed up by the forest.

It was not until the 15th century that people began moving back to Hedalen. There was a story that one day a hunter came into the area. He spotted a grouse perched in a low tree, took aim, and shot – but missed the bird. However, his arrow hit something metal, so he went to investigate. There beneath some large trees stood a little brown church with a small tower beside it. His arrow had hit the bell in the bell tower.

The hunter was very superstitious and believed that the church was the property of the *huldrefolk* (underground people), so he feared the church would disappear if he did not immediately throw an *ildjern* (fire steel) over the church. Of course, the church did not disappear. The hunter cautiously approached and went inside. Up near the altar, there was a bear that had made it its winter home. The hunter killed the bear, skinned it, and fastened the bear hide to the church wall.

And so the story was told to me by my mother when I was a little girl. She said it was a true story because she had seen a piece of the bear hide, as well as a piece of wood from the church, brought by her immigrant ancestors from Valdres to Wisconsin when they arrived there in 1857. I always wanted to see the old artifacts as proof, but it seemed that they had long since disappeared.

In 1965, after my Grandma Dybdahl died, my mother found a little box that contained a small cube of wood and a tiny strip of hide with reddish-brown hair attached to it. She immediately recognized that they were the ancient relics her Norwegian ancestors brought with them from the Hedal church in Valdres. I now have those relics in a display box.

The Bear in the Hedal Church

Hedal Stav Church
Photo by G. Rohlfing

Bearskin (photo by G. Rohlfing) and piece of bear hair

Piece of wood from missing square of Hedal Church portal

After finding the story in a collection of folktales, I wrote to the Hedal Church. Some months later I received a letter from the curator of the church stating:

> *"As to the history or legend from old times about the bear that was shot in or by the church, it is not known if it is true history or not. On the other hand, I know for certain that the bear skin in the vestry at Hedal's church has been there since the 1500s."*

On my first trip to Norway, I was impressed when I first saw the massive front door with immense hand-wrought iron hinges and locks at the Hedal church. I was stunned to see where a square had been cut out of the magnificently carved portal, and then understand that, no doubt, that was the source of the little piece of wood. It seemed unbelievable that my relatives would deface something so precious that had been there since about 1160, but there it was - the missing portion now covered with a flat piece of wood. The bearskin, minus my strip of bear hide, was in the vestry safely preserved behind an old 6-pane window.

Since that first trip to Norway, I have returned to Hedalen many times to stand in the doorway of that medieval edifice and have felt totally blown away to think that at least 20 identified generations of my forefathers walked through that very door for baptisms, confirmations, weddings, funerals, and to worship — and if the legend is true, the old bear waddled through the same doorway to make a den by the altar sometime before 1600.

So why did my ancestors deface the portal? Might the emigrants have considered these bits as a sort of talisman on their journey to America? After many years of searching for an explanation, I have finally reconciled myself to the fact that they did not think of it as defacing anything, since they understood that the church would soon be torn down and replaced with a larger church. My logic is based on the fact that at one time there were hundreds of wooden *stav* churches in Norway, but by 1800 less than 100 remained, many in poor repair, several of them in Valdres. I was told that a law was passed in Norway in 1851, requiring all churches to be large enough to hold 60% of the membership in the parish. A new church was built in the middle 1850s in Begnadal to serve the residents of Lower Hedal, and at the same time, many people were going to America. It is not known if the old church was destined to be demolished, but by some stroke of luck, it was spared. It has been renovated and preserved and serves as a beautiful parish church to the present day.

Mini-history of Norway continued

The last king of the old Norwegian dynasty to rule Norway was Olaf Haakonson, whose mother was the Danish princess, Margaret. Through her efforts, Olaf was elected king of Denmark when he was a small boy. When Olaf's father, Haakon VI, died in 1380, young Olaf became king of Norway as well, bringing about a union with Denmark. In 1387, the young king Olaf died at the age of seventeen years, and his mother Queen Margaret became ruler of Denmark and Norway. The following year she became queen of Sweden as well. She called a meeting of the three Scandinavian countries in

1397, which resulted in the Kalmar Union. This union lasted until Sweden seceded in 1523.

Despite a 1536 declaration that Norway would henceforth be merely a province of Denmark, she remained a kingdom of her own, but without any leadership or power. All important government positions in Norway were occupied by Danish nobles, and the ruler in Denmark had supreme power over Norway. Through the clergy and tax collectors, Norway was constantly reminded of where the power lay. The union of Norway and Denmark lasted until 1814, a period of 400 years.

When the Reformation swept across Europe in the early 1500s, Denmark accepted Lutheranism for its kingdom, which included Norway. By order of the king of Denmark, Norway lost her national church and native clergy in 1536, the same year that the country was stripped of all its power and leadership in government. Monasteries and convents were destroyed, and priests who did not want to become Lutheran clergymen were required to leave the country, never to return. They were replaced by Lutheran clergymen who had been educated in Denmark or Germany.

German merchants of the Hanseatic League began taking control of commerce in Norway as early as the 13th century and continued to be a powerful organization until the end of the 16th century. Although most of the Hansa merchants left Norway when the League was dissolved in 1630, a few remained. They married into the upper classes and raised families. A few German-named clergymen came to Norway, and some of them stayed there and raised families. This explains the presence of German names among Norwegian families. However, the peasant class was rarely affected by outside influences, for seldom were there liaisons between Norwegian peasants and foreigners.

After Oslo was destroyed by fire in 1624, King Christian IV built a new town to the west of the old city and named it Christiania after himself. It retained that name for three centuries, until well after the time when most Americans' ancestors had emigrated. The old name, Oslo, was reinstated in 1924.

Norway's union with Denmark lasted until the end of the Napoleonic Wars in Europe when Denmark was on the losing side. In the settlement following the war, Norway was ceded to Sweden. Norway rose in protest and elected a group of delegates to draft her own constitution. It was at Eidsvoll on May 17, 1814, that this document was adopted, whereby Norway was to become a free, independent, and democratically ruled country. A brief and rather uneventful war with Sweden followed. It lasted only a few days. In the final outcome, Norway was forced to accept the union with Sweden.

The new union gave Norway much more independence than was allowed under Danish rule, and Sweden recognized most aspects of Norway's new constitution. A true feeling of independence reigned. Although their king was in Sweden, certain democratic rights were honored, and the long-dormant potential of the country to run itself came to life. The element of freedom allowed under Swedish rule gave the Norwegian people something they had not known for four hundred years. They had sampled independence, and a new feeling and nationalism prevailed.

Under the new constitution, Norway began to realize a period of increased prosperity, which led to improved living conditions and better nutrition. These advances, along with the introduction of vaccination for smallpox, resulted in a population explosion that the country was not equipped to support. Norway simply could not produce sufficient food to feed its rapidly growing population. Given these circumstances, it is not surprising to find many rural Norwegians "between rocks and hard places" in the first half of the 19th century. Against this background, the seeds of emigration were sown, and in 1825 the first organized boatload of emigrants left Stavanger for America.

It was not until 80 years after the first emigrant group left for America that Norway gained her independence. On June 7, 1905, the union with Sweden was peacefully dissolved, and the Norwegian Parliament invited Prince Carl of Denmark to be the King of Norway. Carl requested a plebiscite to determine whether Norway wanted a republic or monarchy, with the result showing the vast majority in favor of a monarchy.

November 18, 1905, Prince Carl of Denmark became King Haakon VII of Norway. The first time he was to see Norway was when he arrived there as a new king. With him were his wife, Maud (daughter of Edward VII of England), and their two-year-old son, Olav. Haakon VII died in 1957, and his son, Olav V, became King of Norway. When Olav V, King of Norway, died on January 17, 1991, his son, Harald V, succeeded to the throne. Harald is the first prince born in Norway in 566 years, and the first Norwegian-born sovereign to rule in Norway in over 600 years.

Chapter 2

THE NORWEGIAN PEOPLE

Throughout history, Norway has had contact with many other countries, yet she remained totally Norwegian. In Viking times raiding parties from Norway sailed along the coast of Europe into the Mediterranean Sea, to Ireland, Scotland, England, and even into Russia; but little of these other cultures were brought back to Norway with the Vikings. Until recently the only minority group in the country was the Sami (Lapp) population, a small group of nomadic tradition, living mainly in the north of Norway.

In the 13th century, Hansa merchants from Germany established a trading center in Europe. Gradually their influence increased until finally, they had control over all trade. These foreign merchants established a society of their own in the city of Bergen, having little social contact with Norwegians. The monopoly of the Hansa merchants lasted until the middle of the 1500s, and although they left behind evidence of their presence in the city, it had little effect on the rural districts. Clergy, administrative officials, and merchants came to Norway, primarily from Denmark and Germany. Generally, they remained in Norway only until their terms of service ended, at which time they returned to their respective homelands. The local population of common people remained aloof and independent and was not greatly influenced by the presence of any of these foreign elements in their society. In fact, much of the rural population was hardly aware of their presence.

Another factor contributing to the homogenous nature of the Norwegian population is that the country was never conquered or taken over by a foreign government. The forced presence of the Germans from 1940-1945, was the first time in her long history that

Norway had been occupied by a foreign element. This relatively short occupation left little German influence on the character of the Norwegians.

Our forefathers, who emigrated from Norway during the middle 1800s, were born during a time of general prosperity following an economic depression in the early part of that century. Samuel Laing, an Englishman, who lived in Norway for several years in the 1830s, wrote about the circumstances of the people and their reaction to the newly found, conditional independence following their freedom from Danish rule in 1814. From Samuel Laing's *Journal of a Residence in Norway During the Years 1834, 1835, and 1836* published in London in 1837:

> "*They are the most interesting and singular group of people in Europe. They live under ancient laws and social arrangements totally different in principle from those which regulate society and property in the feudally constituted countries, and among them, perhaps, may be traced the germs of all free institutions which distinguish the British constitution to the present day. They present to the political philosopher the singular spectacle of a nation emerging suddenly from under the hand of an uncontrolled and absolute sovereign power, with their civil liberties and social arrangements so well adapted to their condition, and so well secured in their ancient laws, that the transition from despotism to democracy was unmarked by any convulsion or revolutionary movement, or important change in the state of society and property.*
>
> "*There is no circumstance in the condition of the people of this country which strikes the observer more than the great equality of all classes not only in houses, furniture, diet, and the enjoyment of the necessaries and comforts of life, but in manners, habits, and character; They all approach much more nearly to the one standard than in any other country; and the standard is far from being a low one as to character, manners, and habits. In these the educated and cultivated*

*class are, to English feelings at least, far above the higher
classes in other foreign countries."*

There is general agreement among the travelers in Norway from England and America during the 19th century in regard to the character of the Norwegian people. Like Laing, these observers found the great equality of all classes the most striking characteristic. This is due, in part, to the fact that so few were rich that the wealthy had virtually no effect on the population in general. Another quality was hospitality. In the *Poetic Edda*, composed during Viking times, the supreme virtue of the Norsemen was hospitality. This quality is alive and well in Norway today, some ten centuries later.

It is also said that Norwegian people demonstrated only one set of manners which were considered to be habitually good. Courtesy was shown not only to strangers and outsiders but extended within the family unit as well. The Norwegian character was naturally mild, amiable, and free from the anxieties or fears resulting from status-seeking, money-making, and/or money-losing. Apparently, *skynd deg* (hurry up) was a command given only by foreign travelers, and then rarely heeded by Norwegians. Vulgarity existed but was not a common quality found among the people.

Hearing such reports about the people of Norway during the 19th century, it comes as a shock to some when they discover that their ancestors in Norway often had babies before they were married, or at least within the first few months after marriage. Some authorities suggest that this did not happen by accident, nor was marriage a matter of the heart. Inheritance laws at the time made it necessary to have a child to inherit property, so if a man intended to marry, he must first make certain that the woman he took as his wife was capable of producing an heir. It was of great importance to have an heir, not only to inherit the farm and keep it in the family, but to provide security for the farmer and his wife when they got old. The oldest son usually took over the farm, but if there were no sons, a daughter and her husband could fill this role. Whoever took over the farm provided a home and pension for the parents, and the older couple continued to contribute many valuable services to the farm work and household activity as long as they were able.

Not only was it necessary for a farmer's wife to be capable of bearing children and managing a household, but she was also required to do more work on the farm than was commonly expected of women on farms in other parts of Europe. If the husband was a *husmann* (cotter), his labor was required in the land owner's fields. It was up to the wife to tend the fields and flocks at home. If the husband worked in the forests or went to sea for all or part of the year, again, the woman was in charge at home. Dairying had always been "women's work," so there were few jobs on a Norwegian farm that were beyond the capability of a woman. Might this efficiency on the part of Norwegian women be a part of the reason that a law was enacted in 1854, giving women the equal right of inheritance with men?

A typical household of several generations
Axel Lindahl/Norsk Folkemuseum

Casual sleeping arrangements existed among the rural peasant class in the old days. Houses were very small and families large, so the older children in the family slept in the haylofts. In the same lofts young farm laborers of both sexes shared sleeping quarters, so it was not unheard of for a relationship to develop which resulted in a young girl becoming pregnant without the benefit of marriage. Such behavior was not exclusive to this class of people. Members of the upper classes, and even clergymen in some cases, were sometimes overly intimate in their associations with members of the opposite sex.

We are fortunate to have available the findings of Eilert Sundt, a man who was provided with a stipend by the Norwegian Parliament in the mid-1800s for the purpose of studying social conditions in Norway, particularly among the rural class. He and his educated wife traveled extensively observing people in their home communities. They made detailed reports of their findings, particularly in relation to marriage, morals, cleanliness, sobriety, and more. Sundt published three volumes; one each in 1857, 1864, and 1866. His observations are quoted at length in Michael Drake's book, *Population and Society in Norway 1735-1865*, published in 1969.

Eilert Sundt comments that there was a difference in the frequency of illegitimacy from one rural community to another, and this was also noted by the writer, Henrik Wergeland. According to the latter, it was regarded with complete indifference when an unmarried woman had a child in Sogn. This was not the case in Voss, where women who had children out of wedlock were set apart by a special headdress, could not appear on the dance floor at a public dance, and were called "half-wives."

Although Norway had an element of immorality among her people, the high rate of illegitimacy was not exclusively attributable to loose morals. Contributing factors included the postponement of marriage due to poverty, small quarters (especially as relates to sleeping arrangements), ignorance, and sometimes indifference. A great difference in this respect has been noted between advanced and backward areas of Norway.

A great problem facing Norway in the early 1800s resulted from removing restrictions on the manufacture of distilled liquor in the home. After these restrictions were removed in 1816, many family gatherings and celebrations became little more than brawls.

However, not all people in Norway abused the use of liquor. Some of them were extremely pietistic, adhering closely to the teaching of the church of Norway or to the new religious practices advanced by Hans Nielsen Hauge. Hauge was the famous Norwegian lay evangelist who was responsible for the spiritual awakening of Norwegians in the first part of the 1800s.

Before the advent of a formal welfare system in Norway, old, indigent, and poor people were taken care of by their relatives or neighbors. They were given a place to sleep (probably a corner by the fireplace) and were provided with food in return for whatever they were able to do to help out. They often stayed awhile at one place and then moved on to another. According to the census of 1801, many of our forefathers' farms had a *fattiglem* (pauper or beggar) residing there. Some of them might even have been among our relatives!

In 1810 it became a requirement that all Norwegians get a smallpox vaccination. This was the first national program of disease prevention and resulted in its being virtually eliminated within two generations.

The "1810 midwives' code" established qualifications for a network of publicly paid, qualified midwives. The effects of this were not easy to measure, but it is an example of early provisional health care. The Public Law of 16 May 1860 was the beginning of efforts to establish basic principles for preventive and primary health care. Early on it primarily resulted in district medical officers reporting more statistics, but public health remained extremely varied throughout the country.

Among the truly unfortunate in Norway in the 1800s and before, were the lepers. It was surprising to learn that leprosy was one of Norway's most dreaded diseases. It was most prevalent in the fishing districts along the coast of West Norway, though rarely found elsewhere in the country. As early as the Middle Ages, leper hospitals had been established where care was provided for the victims of this disease. In the middle 1800s, there were several leper hospitals in Norway, the largest in Molde, Trondheim, and Bergen. In his book, *Land of the Midnight Sun*, written by Paul DuChaillu, and published in 1881, the author states that three leper hospitals contained, on average, over 2000 lepers. He described the hospitals as very clean, with the men and women separated. A school was maintained at the hospital for children with the disease.

It was a Norwegian physician at the hospital in Bergen, G. Armauer Hansen, who discovered the infectious disease lepra bacillus in 1874, giving leprosy the common name, Hansen's Disease. In 1877 the "Act of the Maintenance of Poor Lepers, etc." was enacted, and in 1885 that legislation was extended by the "Act on the Seclusion of Lepers, etc.." With this patients had to be isolated in separate rooms either at home or in a hospital. Thanks to Hansen's discovery, great strides were made to combat the disease, resulting in its virtual disappearance from Norway early in the 20th century.

DuChaillu tells about other diseases commonly found in Norway:

> "The most prevalent diseases of Scandinavia are scarlatina, typhoid fever, measles, whooping-cough, smallpox (rarely epidemic), diarrhea, dysentery, consumption, pneumonia, and cancer. The cholera first showed itself in 1832, and has since then appeared at varying intervals more or less epidemically. Intermittent and remittent fevers are very rare. Typhoid fever is the most prevalent epidemic."

The Population of Norway

At the end of the Viking Age (ca. 1050) the population of Norway was about 240,000. Prior to the Black Death in 1349, Norway's population estimates ranged from 300,000 to 560,000. It is believed that one-third to one-half of the population succumbed to the plague, leaving an estimated 200,000 survivors. From that time forward the population has grown as follows:

Year	Population
Early 1500s	300,000
Late 1500s	400,000
1700	500,000
1720	530,000
1769	700,000
1801	883,000
1825	1,195,000
1845	1,328,000
1855	1,490,000
1867	1,702,000
1875	1,793,000
1900	2,218,000
1928	2,811,000
1962	3,343,000
1980	4,051,000
1990	4,214,000
2000	4,478,000
2010	4,858,000
2015	5,189,000
2020	5,421,241

Chapter 3

THE NORWEGIAN FARM
AND FARMER

Farm Ownership

Up until the last half of the 1800s, most Norwegians lived on farms and dependent cottages. The farm often had the same name as it had 500 to 1,000 years before, only the spelling and pronunciation changed over the years. Farm boundary lines were defined by existing features of nature, such as mountain ranges, rivers, streams, fjords, seashores, etc. Many of these farms' boundaries are the same today as they were centuries ago. This is especially true of the oldest farms, which were usually large farms. Some of the more recently established farms do not have visible, natural borders.

Until the 1700s, most farmers in Norway did not own the farms they occupied and cultivated but were simply tenants. The king owned about 10% of the farms, the church owned about 40%, the aristocracy had about 15%, and 35% were in private hands. Because the government of Denmark-Norway was in poor financial straits in 1660, large parcels of crown land were sold to rich nobles and burghers in an effort to replenish the empty coffers. The change of property ownership, as it was practiced in Norway, did not alter the condition of the peasants who were renting the land. Until new regulations were established in 1685, which protected tenants from abuse by their proprietors, tenants continued to be exploited by the new property owners. The first reform allowed the sale of individual farms at lower prices than previously making it possible for a tenant farmer to purchase the farm on which he was living. By the year 1723, a proprietor who wanted to sell his property was required by law to give his tenant farmer the right of first refusal to purchase the farm.

Most farms in Norway were made up of several separate units. Large farms might have 80 to 100 residents living in a dozen separate households. In addition to the main farm where the proprietor or freeholder lived, there were rental units, each called a *bruk*, and operated by tenant farmers. It was customary to find one or more *husmann's plass* (cotter's place), located at the fringe of the farm and occupied by sharecroppers. Far up in the mountains was the *seter* (summer farm) where animals were pastured in the summer.

Very strict laws of inheritance were in practice in Norway from early times. The ancient *odelslov* (allodial law), was established during the reign of Magnus Lawmender in the year 1274. According to this law, a farm must have gone through five generations of the same family, and be owned by the sixth generation of that same family, before it became the allodial of the descendants. This system provided for a farm owner's descendants to purchase the family farm upon the death of its owner. The oldest son had the right to buy out his brothers' and sisters' share of the inheritance at a price set by a commission appointed to evaluate the property. (A daughter's share of the inheritance was one-half that of a son). In very early times the direct descendants, as well as any collateral descendants, had the right to repurchase, at any time, a farm that had been sold to a non-relative or outsider. The time limit during which a family member could exercise allodial rights was later set at 20 years. In 1771, it was shortened to 10 years and applied to only direct descendants. In 1856, the redemption time was reduced to 5 years. Modifications and changes in the allodial law (*odelsrett*) have been made from that time to the present, but it is still a form of the old regulations which dictate who has the right to inherit property in Norway. Some regulations were described in *News of Norway*, March 27, 1981:

> "*The Allodial Act gives priority right to the eldest children to take over the family farm, preventing them from being subdivided, and is one of the several acts aimed at promoting a rational farm structure. The Land Act protects farm land and requires arable acreage to be used for agricultural production.*

Partitioning of farms is prohibited. The Concession Act regulates the transfer of real estate and is designed to further protect farming areas. In order to buy a farm a buyer must have the necessary professional qualifications and he must take up residence on the farm and operate it for five years. The Agricultural Development Fund coordinates support for investments in agriculture. It grants funds for drainage and irrigation, construction and major repair of farm buildings and silos, leveling of land, and for replanting of orchards. The Regional Development Fund provides funds for industrial development, enabling farmers to supplement their incomes. The Building and Land Planning Act preserves rural areas for tourism and recreation, another source of income for the local farmer.

In addition to laws which kept family farms within the family, there were laws regulating the cotters' or husmenns' little places. The Husmann's Law of 1851 required tenant farmers to receive the permission of the landowners in order to establish or discontinue any cotter's place which was located on his tenant farm."

Farm Residents

Charles Brace, in *The Norse Folk*, published in 1857, refers to the Norwegian farmer as being of a distinct class and a natural-born prince. His domain was his *gard* (farm), of which, in all likelihood, he became the owner by exercising his allodial rights. The farm had a name permanently attached to it since prehistoric times, and this farm name became a part of the name by which the proprietor was identified. These ancient farm names became the surnames of many families, both in Norway and after emigration to America.

The farming community in Norway was made up of several categories of people. At the top were the farm-owners or free-holders called *bønder* or *gardmenn*. Tenant farmers and owners of small farm divisions were called *brukere*, and the cotter's places at the outer fringe of the farm were occupied by *husmannsfolk*, or "sharecroppers."

A farm laborer, or residing servant at the home of a small land-owner, was known as an *innerst*. Servants at the farm were called *tjenestefolk*. In return for the services they received food, maybe a little money, clothing, and lodging in the hayloft or one of the out-buildings at the farm.

Making Hay
Vesterheim Norwegian-American Museum, Decorah, IA

Not all people were able to find work. Among the unemployed were the *fattiglemmer* or paupers, who went from place to place begging or doing what they could to sustain life.

Much of the work on the farm was done by the *husmannsfolk*. The *husmann* (cotter) was either the younger son of the farm owner, and had no right of inheritance, or was someone who had no money to buy or rent land. He was provided with a small dwelling, maybe a cow, sheep, or a few goats, and sometimes the use of a tiny plot of ground, in return for labor and/or a fee. It was not only the cotter's labor but also that of his wife and children, that was required.

When the cotter's children were 8 or 9 years old they were given chores to do in return for their food. In some districts, boys as young as 8 years of age were given the responsibility of tending sheep and goats at the mountain farm in summer. In addition to their food, these lads were rewarded with a pair of shoes, a cap, and a complete set of clothes. In areas where there was the danger of wild animals threatening the livestock while on the mountain pastures, an older, more responsible boy was employed. His pay usually included a small amount of money in addition to food and clothes.

Boy minding the goats in the seter
Anders B. Wilse/Norsk Folkemuseum

By the time the cotters' children were 12 years old, their work requirements on the farm increased to such an extent that they were provided with both food and clothing. Following confirmation in the state church of Norway, at about 15 years of age, they were considered adults. At that time a cotter's child usually secured a position on the farm as a servant. In the last half of the 19th century, a new opportunity presented itself to these young people. They could consider going to America.

The vast majority of people living in Norway were of the rural class and made their living by farming. These were true agricultural farmers who grew and produced nearly all they needed to eat, drink, wear, and use as tools and equipment on their own property. Near the farm buildings were the fields where grain crops, potatoes, and the best hay were grown. Next were the outfields, where a few crops could be grown and where cattle were pastured.

Farthest from the main farm was the *seter*. Sometimes a farm had two, one closer to home and the other higher up in the mountains where cows, goats, and sometimes sheep and hogs, were pastured in the summer.

Shearing sheep
Vesterheim Norwegian-American Museum, Decorah, IA

Another type of farm was that found in the mountains. The mountain farmer depended on the forests and cattle to provide a living. He lived at the very edge of the agricultural area or entirely in the mountains. These farmers were the most rustic, and predictably retained the character, costume, dialect, and other customs from ancient times, and were the least affected by outside influences.

A third kind of farm was found on the coast and in the fjords. Fishermen-farmers had small farms and were dependent on fishing for their main sustenance. In addition, they often had sheep or goats and raised a few crops.

Many farmers were also good at crafts, trades, lumbering, building boats and ships, and dealing in livestock, combining these occupations with farming.

Farm Buildings

Almost all buildings on a Norwegian farm, as well as all furnishings, containers, fittings, tools, and utensils used there, were constructed of wood. This included carts, wagons, and farm implements, and also furniture in the dwelling house. Not only was everything made of wood, but it was also made by residents at the farm where it was used.

In most European countries, peasants lived in villages and went out to the fields to work. In Norway, peasants lived on the land they farmed. The peasants or farmers of Norway were competent in many areas besides those of a purely agricultural nature. Some were tanners, carpenters, blacksmiths, woodcarvers, or were proficient in other skills that were required for the operation of a farm. Therefore, the farm had to consist not only of dwellings and shelters for animals but also of buildings where the various crafts and trades could be carried out.

The buildings on a Norwegian farm were arranged around an open area or farmyard called the *tun*. In English, the word is "town," pronounced much the same as the Norwegian *tun*. Arrangement of buildings around the open yard depended upon the topography of the land as well as on the number of buildings located there. The buildings might be arranged around a closed square, an open square, a row, or in a cluster. In some areas, such as Gudbrandsdal, one finds the double *tun*, with the dwelling and storehouses located around one yard, and the outbuildings around the other. Often it was the established tradition in a particular district that dictated the type of *tun*, with allowance made for the terrain. Whatever form the *tun* presented, it contained the dwelling house of the farmer, storehouses, animal shelters, and other structures necessary to the operation of a self-sufficient farm.

Norwegian Farm Buildings
Vesterheim Norwegian-American Museum, Decorah, IA

Placement of buildings within the *tun* depended on function. Level plots of ground were kept for raising crops, and the buildings were located on hillsides or mountain slopes nearby. Dwellings and storehouses were almost always located on a dry spot where the sun shone, and at the top of the slope above the out-buildings. The cow barn was usually located the farthest down the slope, so that seepage from the manure pile would fertilize the fields below.

The Stabbur

It was vital to the operation of the farm to have a secure dry place to store food and supplies for the people and animals living there. This was provided by the *stabbur* or *loft*, structures unique to rural Norway. Although most dwelling houses lacked decoration, the *stabbur* or *loft* was often decorated with elaborate carving on the door and/or corner posts.

Stabbur

The *stabbur* and *loft* were unheated storehouses of one or two stories, built on pillars. Not only did the pillars keep the contents of the building dry, but they also prevented rodents and vermin from reaching what was stored inside. The building might have a gallery on one or more sides of the lower floor, which was reached by stone or wooden steps. The steps were detached from the gallery, leaving a gap of such width that a human could easily step across to the gallery, but unwelcome creatures could not.

If the storehouse had a second story it extended over the first and often had a balcony around one or more sides. The second floor was reached by a wooden stairway from the gallery below to the balcony above.

Inside the lower floor of the building were stores of grain, flat-bread, meat, flour, and provisions for the farm which were stored in large wooden bins or vessels. This floor might also be used for sleeping during the summer. Guests were housed there when a wedding, confirmation, baptism, or funeral took place at the farm. Most of the winter stores would have been consumed and the room would be quite empty until the fall harvest. The second floor was used for storing clothes, bedding, and equipment; as well as for spinning and weaving in the summer. It might also be used by guests, and sometimes servant girls, as sleeping quarters during the summer.

Stabbur in Rauland
Vesterheim Norwegian-American Museum, Decorah, IA

Many storehouses were not the romanticized little houses on stilts with carved decorations but were utilitarian and simple storehouses built on the ground. A structure of this type might be called a *bu*.

Out Buildings

In addition to dwelling houses and storehouses, many "out-houses" were commonly found at each farm in Norway. Most farm buildings were small and housed only one kind of animal or had only one function. Since most herds and flocks were not large, their houses need not be huge. Although Norwegians had the expertise to construct very large out-buildings using notched horizontal logs, it was more practical to build many small buildings. Trees were of limited height, yielding a log of limited length for building, so construction was done in the most functional way.

Generally, each type of animal had its own house, but occasionally the pig house was connected to the horse barn, sheep might have a pen in the cow barn, or the cow barn was located under the hay barn. The following buildings were among those found on the farm.

Låve or *trev* – hay barn with a threshing floor. Each farm had one or more hay barns. They were most often located near the stable and cow barn. Wagon loads of hay, grain crops, and other fodder were hauled up an inclined driveway to the floor of the *låve*. The center of the floor was used for threshing grain, and the straw, hay, and other fodder were stored on either side of the threshing floor. Sometimes horses and wagons were also kept in the haybarn.

Fjøs – cow barn. The cow barn was located below the other buildings on the farm, and a hole in the floor allowed the manure to be pushed out to a dung pit under the barn. Seepage from the dung heap fertilized the fields below the barn. In the spring manure was spread on the fields not only for fertilizing, but to speed the thawing of snow.

Tørkehus – drying house. The drying house was equipped with a kiln to dry grain for threshing, as well as malt, hemp, and flax. The material to be dried was spread on the floor and heat from the kiln served to reduce the moisture content of the produce. Like the blacksmith shop and cook house, the drying house was located away from other buildings.

Edlhus – Cook house. It was here that washing, brewing, and baking were done. Like the blacksmith shop and drying house, it was located away from the other buildings.

Stall – stable or horse barn. Hay was sometimes stored above the horse barn.

Grisehus – pig house

Sauehus or *smalefjøs* – sheep house

Geitehus – goat house

Hønsehus – hen house

Skytje or *vedhus* – woodshed. Storehouse for firewood, wood for building and fencing.

Redskapsbu – tool shed

Potetkjeller –potato cellar

Naust – boathouse

Do – privy

Smie – blacksmith shop. The blacksmith shop was located away from other buildings because of the danger of fire. It contained a forge, sheepskin bellows, and anvil.

Kvern – mill. Mills were located on the stream nearest the farm and were used in spring and fall when the water supply was plentiful. There were mills for sawing lumber, grinding flour, and for fulling wool. Many farms had their own mill. Others were shared by several farms.

The Seter

The *seter hus*, or *sel*, was a mountain hut built in the remote pastures which were located quite a distance from the main farm. It was usually located near a mountain stream. In early summer animals were grazed fairly near the farm, but by midsummer, they were pastured in the mountains. This was too far from the farm to bring the milk home every day, so it was necessary to make cheese and butter at the *seter* in the mountain. A responsible woman was left at home to manage the household, and another woman (often the housewife) who was especially talented at making cheese and butter, went with the animals and some of the younger women and children to the mountains where they spent the entire summer. The youngest of those at the *seter* was responsible for herding the animals in the mountain pastures. The animals came when called by the herd girl, and they more frequently followed her than were driven. Sometimes it was necessary to hire a boy to assist in herding the animals.

Older girls were milkmaids and helped process the milk into butter and cheese. This was done with care, as their expertise (or lack of it) was evident at mealtimes all winter long. Some dairy maids believed that it was necessary to have magic symbols carved or burned into their churn and containers. They believed the magic power of the symbols assured a quality product and preserved the butter and cheese.

On weekends the father, or someone else from the farm, took provisions to the mountain farm on a packhorse and brought home the containers of cheese and butter which were made during the week.

Life in the mountains during the summer could be very enjoyable as well as a busy time. Sometimes the mountain cabins were in clusters so a lot of visiting went on between the people spending the summer there. On Saturday nights young people, and others from the home farms in the district, would gather in the mountains where they would have music for dancing and enjoy the good food prepared with fresh milk.

Milking goats in the seter
Vesterheim Norwegian-American Museum,
Decorah, IA

Even in the southern part of Norway sunset came very late, and nighttime lasted for only a few hours in midsummer. As fall approached the days shortened, and soon it was time to take the animals home. They were left out in a pasture near the farm for a while before being put in the barn for the winter. According to old tradition, all people and animals should be home from the summer pastures in the mountains in time for St. Bartholomew's Eve, August 24th. The master of the farm usually had good porridge as well as plenty to drink for everyone at the farm. It was customary to mark the completion of an important part of the farm work, such as haying, harvesting, and bringing animals home from the *seter*, with a celebration of thanksgiving. Norwegian peasants eagerly anticipated these times of celebration.

Crop Failures

In the middle of the 18th century, Norway experienced an extended period of crop failures. In an effort to relieve the suffering of the rural people, new agricultural methods and new crops were introduced. One of the most important new crops was the potato. From *A History of Norway*, by Karen Larsen:

> "...the clergy especially tried to spread the new methods among the people. They came to be known as 'potato priests.' And the farmers were learning. Although suspicion of everything new lingered long, there were many intelligent leaders among the people. Hardanger and Sogn became especially famous for their orchards. Although there was steady progress... life on the farm continued much as of yore."

Conditions became desperate when there were four successive years of severe crop failures. Concerning these years Karen Larsen wrote:

> "In spite of progress Norway continued to be dependent upon importation of grain, and a most serious cause of complaint was the Danish monopoly of this trade. Nothing short of a famine could procure a change. Four successive crop failures

from 1739 through 1742, the 'black years' as they are called, brought upon Norway the greatest calamity of this age. The grain trade was temporarily freed and measures of relief were taken, but the bureaucracy moved slowly, and the food needed was not obtainable. The governor of Christiania wrote: 'This year [1742] I have with deep sorrow seen hundreds of people from the Uplands here in the city looking for work; but we have had nothing for them to do. So they have walked homewards, and some have perished on the way.'"

Peas, potatoes, barley, rye, and flax crops were often in danger of failure because of Norway's short summer. During the Napoleonic War (1807-1814) the country experienced three particularly bad years. Failures in the grain harvest were recorded in 1807, 1808, and 1812. At the same time, England blockaded Norwegian ports, preventing a supply of grain from reaching the Norwegian people. According to Carl Narvestad in *Valdres Samband 1899-1974*, pages 24-26:

"In 1812 Valdres had the poorest crop recorded. The grain crop froze early in the summer and people ate a meal of moss and the bark of the birch, elm and willow. Folk became so undernourished that when they finally got barley meal their bodies could not tolerate the 'rich' diet and health authorities advised people not to make an abrupt change in their eating habits. In 1817, too, crops froze causing great hardship."

The end of the war did not mean the end of suffering for the masses. The new ruling powers levied heavy taxes, creating a financial burden many were unable to bear. Narvestad continues:

"The poor crop years came at a time when the country was under the burden of new and heavier taxes. The government claimed it was necessary to collect high taxes in order to establish a stable government, but the farmers became restless and resented what they considered unfair demands. The Storting (parliament) was regarded as an implement to help the great and powerful, to suck riches out of the land and ruin folk and country. There were also foreign agitators

at work. They aroused farmers in Ringerike, Hedemarken, Hallingdal and Valdres to revolt against the government. While the movement was stronger elsewhere, it was active in Valdres also, especially around Hedalen.

In Hedalen the church bells were rung to call the masses together. Thore Bertilrud was a leader of the farmers in the uprising and he drilled them on a sandy flat below Grøv.

In Bagn there was a strong feeling against Storting and unrest prevailed for a short time. Agitators were sent to all the upper communities too, all the way to Vang, but these errands bore no fruit."

The minister in Valdres, Hans Jacob Stabel, wrote a letter to King Carl Johan in Sweden, pleading for the people of his parish. It was through his efforts that an apparent uprising was quieted in Valdres. His letter of 1819 stated:

"Most people have had no grain, meal, or bread for three or four weeks and scarcely twenty percent of the best farmers in the parish are able to seed their land this year because they lack seed and cannot obtain the necessary money to purchase seed with."

In the late 1830s crops were again so poor that the people of Valdres once more had to eat moss, bark, and grass. According to Narvestad, a meal was made of moss, sorrel, and certain leaves. The mixture was finely ground and the bitter taste leached out with water, after which it was made into mush or bread.

Crops failed again in the summer of 1860. Rain fell almost continuously through the summer causing severe flooding, washing out sawmills, grist mills, and bridges, creating great hardship for the people of lower Valdres.

Farming has never been an easy occupation in Norway. The limited amount of tillable land, primitive farm tools and implements, and uncertain weather conditions made rural life difficult enough; but in the 19th century, when the population of Norway virtually exploded, conditions became unbearable on many farms. It became necessary to divide and subdivide farms to provide places for everyone. Eventually, the farms became so small that they were no longer able to support the people and animals living there, particularly in years when crops failed.

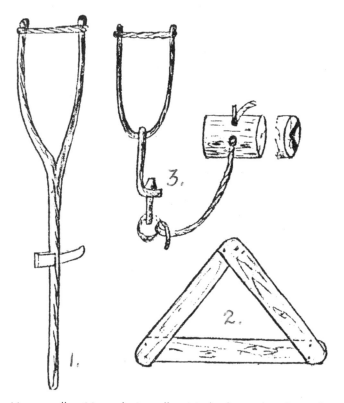

Horse collar (1), and pig collar (2), both used to keep the animals from going through fences. (3) Halter for tying cows. From *Hadeland Bygdebok IV*

There was often a shortage of grain, which was hard on both people and animals. Animals were essential to the livelihood of the community, as they were the main source of food. Fodder for the livestock during bad times included moss, bark, leaves, and twigs from certain trees and bushes, heather, and whatever else might be available to supplement a meager supply of hay and grain.

When cows did not give milk and were left tied in their stalls in the barn, it took less feed to keep them alive. It was also important that as many cows as possible were kept alive through the winter so that the farmer would have an adequate herd in the spring. When the harvest was meager, animals were short-fed; they were given only enough fodder to keep them alive. When the people were often hungry and weak, it was not considered cruel to let some of the animals on the farm go hungry too. Cattle that had been short-fed during the winter were often so weak in the spring that they needed help to walk out of the barn. Those not weakened by lack of food became so excited, jumping and kicking about, so there was danger of breaking legs on an uneven barn floor. It was often necessary for two men, one on each side of the creature, to keep it under control until it was safely outside.

The best fodder on the farm was reserved for the horses, as a horse could not work without being fed, and horses were needed as much in winter as in the summer. The value of a horse was also much greater than that of a cow. It was very important to save some of the best grain from the harvest to be used for seed. If there was a short crop, it was doubly important that enough of the grain be put aside to use for seed in the spring.

Work on the Farm

Everyone from the youngest children to the old folks had duties on the farm. Men were in charge of the fields and forest, while women were in charge of the house and supervised work at the farm. This included care of the farm animals, milking, making butter and cheese, butchering, spinning, weaving, making clothes, helping in the fields, and providing the farm with heirs! When men were away from the farm on hunting or fishing expeditions or to attend the market in Christiania (Oslo), a woman's responsibility on the farm was especially great. Most farms were small and cultivation of even very small fields was difficult. Unpredictable weather made it imperative that a farmer made hay while the sun shone, and used everyone on the farm to help him get the farm work done.

Each farm was nearly self-sufficient as the climate and season allowed. Some years it was necessary to purchase some grain; but often, when Norway was short of grain, other countries had crop failures also, making this foreign source unreliable. When outside help was needed on the farms, work parties were organized and payment was food, drink, and maybe a dance. Another time when the neighbors were called upon to help was when animals were lost. If they were not found, a collection might be taken to give the owner of the missing animal.

Farm equipment

It was essential for the farmer to have a means of noting the passage of time. For this, they depended on "calendar sticks." They were made of wood in a variety of shapes and sizes. Some were round, but most were made from a long narrow stick much like today's yardstick or meter stick. A small carved notch on the surface of the stick denoted each day, and larger notches marked the weeks. Few people could read, but everyone was familiar with the meaning of symbols on a calendar stick. Special symbols indicated special feast or holy days. One side of the stick was the summer side, showing April 14 through October 13. The other side was the winter side, showing October 14 through April 13. The Saint's days continued to be noted, but the less important ones gradually evolved into days marking agriculture activities on the farm so that they would know when to plant crops, take animals to the mountain pastures, harvest the grain, and do other seasonal work. Each district had its own symbols for the various holy days observed. There is more information about the calendar stick in Chapter 9.

Animals were bred so that their young would be born in the spring before it was time to take the animals to their summer pastures at the *seter*. In this way, milk production was at its peak at the time when grazing was the best, and the cows dried up in the fall when they were put in the barn for the winter.

It was the practice to sprinkle dirt or manure on the snow in the spring so as to speed the thawing process and facilitate preparing the ground for planting. Hoes, spades, and plows were used to break up the soil, manure was worked into it with a rake or harrow, and then the seeds were sown or planted. In places where mills relied on floodwater for power, spring was the time for grinding any grain that was left after saving out the seed to be used in planting the fields. Sheep were sheared for their winter wool, fences mended, and all gates closed. According to tradition, animals should no longer be fed inside after May 3rd but should

Norwegian Plough.

a, Sole, flat and of wood.   *b*, Mould-board plated with iron ; and *c*, share ; both fastened to the sole with bolts.   *d*, Regulator, of which the lower part, *e*, touches the ground. *f*, Handle, generally wanting.

be put out to graze in the nearby pastures. May 15th was considered the best time to sow grain.

There was a lull in farm activities after the crops were growing and gates were up to keep the animals out of the fields. This was a time when the house was cleaned thoroughly to get rid of the smoke and dirt from the winter (a good time to have a wedding!). The men checked and repaired roofs and the hay-drying racks. Cows, sheep, goats, and pigs were taken to the mountain pastures, where good grazing conditions fattened them up and assured good milk production from the cows and goats.

Back at the farm, hay was cut and put on racks. When it was dry, the hay was carried by hand or loaded into hay carts and hauled to the hay barn. The carts were small and built very low to the ground, with small wheels to minimize the danger of tipping on the steep slopes. In late summer the grain was cut with a sickle and bound into bunches before being put on poles to dry. When it was dry, it was carried inside and placed in bins where it was safe from birds, mice, and rats, until the time came for threshing.

Harvesting and farm buildings
Vesterheim Norwegian-American Museum, Decorah, IA

As mentioned earlier, animals should be home from the mountain pastures in time for St. Bartholomew's day, August 24th, and certainly no later than September 14th. By this time the grain must be in and gates taken down. It was time to gather twigs and leaves from trees for extra fodder, and the time to gather nuts, herbs, and apples, as well as the time to shear summer wool from the sheep. A second crop of hay was cut and dried before taking it into the barn. This was also the time to butcher animals that could not be kept over the winter and store the meat which was salted and cured. Late in the fall, when it was cold enough so that the grain separated easily from the straw, grain harvesting was done.

By the end of October, all animals were to be fed inside, where they remained in their respective stalls or houses until spring. Since milk production was minimal or non-existent in winter, women were able to concentrate on inside work, making candles, spinning, weaving, knitting, mending, etc. The men made and repaired tools, utensils and equipment, and cut wood for fuel and building. By the sign on the calendar stick, wood for tools must be cut before January 20, as after that time the sap began to rise in the tree. If by the beginning of February there was still one-half of the winter supply of fodder left in the barn, there would be no shortage of fodder for the animals in the spring.

Fishing in the Inner Valleys

Fishing has always been an important activity in Norway, not only along the coast but in the mountains and inner valleys as well. Most farms were close to a body of water. It was also desirable to locate the farm's *seter* (summer dairy) near a stream, not only for refrigeration of dairy products but as a source of fish. Trout, perch, white fish, char, carp, etc., were found in abundance in the lakes, rivers, and streams, and this resource provided an important supplement to the people's food supply and income. Fish not used by the family was sold or traded for other goods.

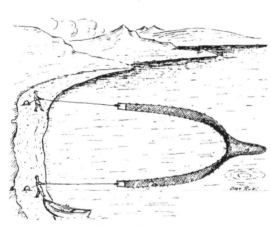

Net fishing from shore

In the fall, when the flow of water was naturally diminished, streams and some rivers were dammed up so the fish gathered in small pools. Torches and lanterns could be used to lure the fish to the edge of the pool where they were caught by hand, clubbed, or speared. Fishing spears were long poles with a forked end having several tines, barbed at the ends. The fish pole with a line and a hook baited with earthworms or small fish was commonly used. Some fishermen used nets and seines which yielded large catches of fish. Ice fishing was popular in winter.

Earthworms were dug in the fall and placed in wooden worm boxes (pictured here). These containers were filled with dirt and stored in a place where they would not freeze providing a winter supply of bait. Fish caught in winter were frozen and thawed as needed, but those caught at other times were used fresh or preserved by salting or drying.

Worm box

A popular means of preserving trout in Valdres was the preparation of *rakauer*, a partially fermented form of fish. The usual method of preparing fish was to boil it and use the heads and skin for soup.

The regular use of fish in the diet of our Norwegian ancestors helps to explain the popularity of fish in the menu of Norwegian-American church suppers and other Norwegian-American organizations. Right up to the present time, many descendants of Norwegian immigrants use fish, particularly *lutefisk*, for the family's traditional Christmas dinner.

The Peasant Army in Norway

It seems out of place to include the military in a discussion of farms and farmers, yet that was the milieu from which soldiers came, and also the setting in which they were trained.

The Norwegian army was a sort of militia made up of unmarried peasants. They drilled several times a year, usually at the churchyard or at the farm of the officer in charge of the army in that particular district. It was first organized in 1628, and was made up of some of the healthiest, tallest, strongest, and smartest of the rural population; one from each of the larger farms, or one from a group of smaller farms. Foot soldiers were required to serve for ten years and cavalrymen twelve years. Soldiers were not generally allowed to marry while in the army unless they could prove that they had the means to support a wife and family.

It was considered an honor to serve in the Norwegian army, and soldiers were held in high esteem in the community. They were to be honored at all gatherings ahead of other men. Military law, not local law, applied to men who were members of the Norwegian army.

Horses could also be conscripted for army service, Samuel Laing tells:

Engebret Nilsen, Fanejunkar in the Norwegian Army born 1844 in Etnedal.

"Every farm of certain size must provide a horse for artillery or cavalry; but as it is paid for by the government while in service, it is considered an advantage rather than a tax."

When Napoleon began breathing down Denmark's neck in the early years of the 19th century it was necessary to increase the army of Norway. No longer could the Norwegians send only the chosen recruits to fulfill their military obligation to Denmark's army. Additional men from the farm census rolls were also conscripted by Danish authorities. When Denmark became actively involved in the Napoleonic War from 1807-1814, every able-bodied Norwegian male was ordered to serve in the army on the side of Napoleon.

Following Napoleon's defeat in 1814, the army was greatly reduced, and most fortifications were abandoned. Norway was then under the authority of Sweden. New rules regarding the selection of soldiers were enacted, whereby they were recruited from the entire male population, not just from the rural population.

Proper way to perform a kick-turn on skis
according to a 1760 military manual.

Chapter 4

HOMES OF RURAL NORWAY

Most dwelling houses in rural Norway were of a similar design and built to last for many generations, if not for centuries. They consisted of a one or two-story building of log construction with a few small windows and either a slate roof or one made of birch bark and sod. Frame construction was used to make the balcony or vestibule, and also for walls separating inside rooms.

Husmannsplass in Sogn
Anders B. Wilse/Norsk Folkemuseum

At one time, houses consisted of one room with a dirt floor and a center fireplace with no chimney or windows. Smoke exited through a smoke hole in the center of the roof. In these houses, the walls were often black with soot. Gradually improvements were made so that by the 17th century a corner fireplace (*peis*) with a chimney was added, making it possible to have a two-story house. Dirt floors were covered with wooden planks, and glass became available making it possible to add windows. Improvements came slowly, but by the end of the 18th century, most houses in rural Norway had a chimney, windows, and wooden floors. Interior walls were left unpainted or were whitewashed, and occasionally were decorated with rosemaling or woven wall hangings. Instead of using rugs or carpets, the green tips of fir or juniper trees were spread on the floors in order to keep the mud and dirt on shoes from soiling them, and also to freshen the air.

Among the smallest and crudest dwellings were those of *husmenn*, described in *Hadeland Bygdenes Historie IV*, 1953. According to that source, a typical *husmannsstue* was only about 12 to 14 feet long and 9 feet wide, with two small windows on the south side and one on the west. A closet for food and clothing took up 3 or 4 feet from the length of the house, leaving the rest for living. The roof was made of birch bark and sod and was so low that one had to stoop to enter through a small door on one side of the house.

Layout of a typical farm house

The most common dwelling house of rural Norway consisted of a large room called a *stue,* and two small rooms; one called the *sval* (entryway) and the other a kammer or kove (storeroom or sleeping room). Some houses also had a half-loft which was used for sleeping and storage. Wooden buckets, casks, boxes, chests, and other containers for food storage were found in the storeroom and entry. Two-story houses had the same arrangement on the first floor, with the second floor providing additional sleeping and storage space.

In some districts, a tar cross was painted on the door of the house. This insured protection against certain supernatural beings, such as "Christmas riders," who came soaring through the air on horseback during the Christmas season. In other districts, it was important that dwelling houses had a special room without windows or doors on outside walls. This was for use as a "birthing room." In old days, some people believed that it was necessary to take every precaution so that *huldrefolk* (wicked, alluring women with cow-like tails) would not get in the room when a baby was born, for they might exchange one of their own *hulder* babies for the newly-born Norwegian baby. Anyone with a deformity, or lacking in the usual facilities of a normal person, was often said to be such a changeling.

Farmhouse showing framskap, benches, corner cupboard, and table

When building a house, Norwegian peasants often numbered the timbers so that they could easily dismantle the building and move it to another location. In my research, I often found families who moved their house. The fact was that the entire building was dismantled, moved, and rebuilt at another location. This was especially true in the case of cotters' houses.

The *peis*, or corner fireplace with a chimney, provided heat and a place to do the family cooking. Furnishings were arranged around the walls of the house, leaving the center of the room clear for carrying out household activities such as spinning and weaving.

Nearest the entrance door was the *framskap* (cupboard) which was under the direct supervision of the housewife. A long table stood along the gable

Framskap or cupboard from Vågå, Gudbrandsdal, ca. 1800. Carved by Jakob Rasumussen Sæterdalen (a carver best known for his work on the pulpit in the Lom stave church) and painted by Peder Olsen Veggum. *Vesterheim – LC 1613.*

wall, with a long bench built into the wall, above which were usually a couple of windows. From the end of the bench and along the wall at one end of the table was the *høgsete* (high seat), where the head of the household sat. His most valuable possessions were kept in a corner cupboard near his seat. Along one of the other walls could be found the bed or beds.

The beds were wide and short, as was common at that time in Norway. They were box-like affairs filled with straw and covered with canvas-like cloth. Most people slept under sheepskins or quilts filled with sedge grass, shredded rags, feathers, or eider-down. Old people and guests were afforded the honor of sleeping under down or feather quilts. Pillows were filled with the same materials as quilts. Younger members of the family slept in the hayloft or in the store-

Corner Bed

Clock in Valdres. *Made by Erland Knutsen Landsend.*

Interior of a home. Carding and spinning
Vesterheim Norwegian-American Museum, Decorah, IA

house, and sometimes in the barn, where it was warmer than in the unheated storehouse.

Other furnishings in the house included a cradle (sometimes hung from the ceiling to conserve space), benches, stools or chairs, a spinning wheel, and a loom. Toward the end of the 1700s, peasants began building *stueklokker,* or living room clocks. They were similar to grandfather clocks and became an important part of home furnishings.

In *Journal of a Residence in Norway,* published in 1837, Samuel Laing describes furnishings and activity going on in the home of rural Norwegian gentry:

> *"The floor is sprinkled with fresh bright green leaves, which have a lively effect; everything is clean and shining; an eight-day clock stands in one corner, a cupboard in another; benches and straight-backed chairs ranged around the room; and all family occupations are going on, exhibiting curious and interesting contrasts of ancient manners, with modern refinement, and even elegance. Carding of wool or flax is going on in one corner; two or three spinning in one corner; two or three spinning wheels are at work near the stove; and a young lady will get up from these old-fashioned occupations, take her guitar in the window seat, and play and sing, or gallopade the length of the room with a sister, in a way that shows that these modern accomplishments have been as well taught as the more homely accomplishments."*

Weaving in Telemark
Vesterheim Norwegian-American Museum, Decorah, IA

E. N. Anderson, an American visitor in Norway, reported his observations in a book, Six Weeks in Norway, published in 1877:

> *"Beautifully carved chests, hanging shelves, and smaller household articles of wood, made by the farmer during the long winter evenings,*

may be seen in even the poorest home. And many of the peasants are skillful workers of iron, while some will give to their steel knives the temper of the Damascus blade."

Carving by Norsk Wood Works Ltd

Families who were better off financially had slightly larger and better houses which might be more elaborately furnished, but the differences from class to class varied little among rural people in Norway in the early and middle nineteenth century. Furnishings in the house were similar, if not identical, in most houses of a given district. The vast majority of Norwegian peasants lived in simple log houses with simple furnishings until the latter part of the 19th century, or even into the 20th century. Many of these dwellings are now used as summer homes by descendants of former residents.

Food and Drink

From travelers' accounts, one concludes that sour milk, *graut* (mush), *flatbrød* (flatbread), and dried meat were some of the mainstays of a Norwegian's diet in the 1800s. They reported that peasants' houses were very simple and sparsely furnished; but in spite of their humble circumstances, rural Norwegians were a most hospitable lot.

As early as 1799, a traveler wrote of his experiences in Norway. He mentioned a supper at 6:00 not being of the regular form, but in the form of sandwiches – *smørbrød* with cheese, perhaps.

Sir Humphrey Davy was a guest at a country house near Oslo in 1824. He was served anchovy, kipper, salmon, brown bread, and butter as appetizers, following which he had ham, peas, cabbage, salmon, chicken, veal, cucumbers, cranberry jelly (probably lingonber-

Serving board with acanthus carving by Ed Barsness

ry), fruit, cakes, cheese, and sweet things. He was not an ordinary traveler and was being entertained in the home of one of the heads of society in the Oslo area. It is certain that this was not the common diet in the country districts of Norway.

In a traveler's anthology, *Travelers Discovering Norway in the Last Century*, Charles Elliott reported on a trip to Norway in 1832. He described his breakfast of husky rye cakes, smoked bacon, and cream.

In the same anthology William Williams said:

"We ate a plastic composition which looked like roman cement, out of a wooden bowl, by dipping wooden spoons into it by turns. The bowl is oblong and contains about an ordinary shovelful. The dirty man sucked his knife and presented it to me with a sweeping bow. One of the girls licked another knife and put it away, nice and clean. I was offered flatbread and rusty raw bacon (probably spike kjøtt), ate a few square feet of flatbread and left the bacon. Next I was handed a wooden tankard, holding about 3 quarts with a wooden cover and holding beer. The dirty man had just drunk from it so I asked for water and was brought a basin full – exactly like the ones supplied for washing."

Because of the importance placed on food and its consumption in many Norwegian-American families, it is interesting to learn about the food habits of our forefathers. It seems that no matter how great or small the event, food was a central focus. When someone dropped in, coffee was served; when a baby was born, *rommegrøt* (cream porridge) was brought to the new mother; when a couple got married, much food, including a big marriage feast was served;

when a person died, food began to arrive in the home of the survivors and feasting followed.

It is not difficult to understand a seeming preoccupation with food in a country that often experienced crop failures that resulted in shortages of food. In a society where people were hungry much of the time, an adequate food supply came to be looked upon as a luxury. There was a certain pride in being fortunate enough to have food to share, and it was a sign of hospitality to offer food to whoever came to one's house. Tradition dies hard among many ethnic groups, and Norwegians are no exception. I sincerely be-

Melkeringe
Vesterheim Norwegian-American Museum, Decorah, IA

Smørøskje (Bentwood butter box)
Vesterheim Norwegian-American Museum, Decorah, IA

lieve that our custom of offering hospitality, food, and drink, to all who come to our homes, originated long ago among our ancestors in Norway.

Food was the same for all those living on the farm. Most farms in Norway had cows and/or goats, making milk and milk products an important part of the diet. Cow's milk was seldom used before it was sour, especially in the summer when the cattle were pastured in the mountains. A *melkeringe* (milk tub) was a container used when the milk was to stand for the cream to separate or to sour. Sweet cheese, sour cheese, cottage cheese, and special cheeses such as *gammeløst* and *primøst*, were made from cow's milk; white and brown cheese was made from goat's milk. Butter, made from cow's milk, was stored in bentwood *smørøskje* (butter box).

Barley was the biggest grain crop raised for food and some rye was used. Oats were raised on some farms, but in the old days, it was believed to be suitable only for horse food.

Wooden serving pieces (21st Century)

The typical diet of a Norwegian did not vary much from one district to the other. The amount of fish or meat eaten depended on the location of the farm, otherwise, food in rural Norway consisted mainly of sour milk, dark bread, cheese, butter, fish, pork, mutton, and potatoes (introduced from England or Scotland about 1750). *Graut* or *grøt* (mush) was common among all Norwegians. It was not the *rommegrøt* that we make from thick cream and wheat flour today, but a more utilitarian mixture of coarse barley flour and water (or milk), served with sour milk or butter – according to the economic conditions of the household. Oatmeal or rye meal was occasionally used, and in some areas mush, in one form or another, was eaten two and three times a day. In addition to using cow's and goat's milk, there were times when the milk from sheep was also used.

In most areas of Norway, people ate four times a day. *Frokost* (breakfast), consisting of coffee and some sort of bread or other food, was eaten first thing in the morning. *Dugurd* was a sort of second breakfast, eaten in late forenoon, and consisted of porridge made from water and barley meal, and sometimes flatbread with cheese. Another meal was eaten at *nonetid*, about 3:00 or 4:00 in the afternoon. Foods commonly served at this meal included dried meat, fish, boiled potatoes, lefse, pork, sausage, and dumplings; but if the family was very poor, they probably had only potatoes. The last meal of the day was *kvelds* (supper), served in the early evening, and consisted of *graut* (mush) and sour milk.

With their meals, people drank water and light beer, as well as whey and buttermilk mixed with water. In the first half of the 1800s coffee was introduced, and soon replaced other drinks in many Norwegian households.

Potatoes, turnips, peas, and onions were important food crops. They were cooked together with meat in the form of stew. Turnips were cooked and mashed to serve with flatbread for supper. The turnip was largely replaced by the potato which came into its own during the famine years from 1807-1814 and added nutritional value to the diet of Norwegian farmers. After about 1820 it became common to serve potatoes when meat or fish was served. Along with eating it cooked by itself, it was added to flatbread, porridge, pancakes, potato cakes, and dumplings (*potet klub*). A coarse flour was ground from the rye and barley grown in Valdres. This was used to make bread and cakes. Sometimes a bit of white flour was purchased to make special breads, as well as *strull, krumkake, goro,* and other baked items for special occasions; but wheat was very expensive and rarely used.

Strull/Krumkake iron
Vesterheim Norwegian-American Museum, Decorah, IA

Flatbread was a staple that was eaten by most people in Norway. It was a flat unleavened bread, which was rolled thin to make large

rounds that were baked on a griddle over an open fire. Some farms had special baking ladies come to the farm, where they spent up to 8 days making flatbread. It was hard and dry and would keep for several years.

William Williams described *flatbrød* as a circular disc about 18 to 20 inches in diameter, and that a hungry man, who is fond

Flatbread box
Vesterheim Norwegian-American Museum,
Decorah, IA

of it, could consume a considerable acreage at one meal.

Lefse was also made, some from potatoes and some from flour; but it was made more delicate than *flatbrød* so was used only on special occasions. It was not possible to make raised bread from barley or oat flour, for neither contain gluten, without which bread dough cannot rise. Flour was ground at the mill in the spring and in the fall. What was needed between times was ground by hand. To make flour last longer, dried elm bark was ground and added to

Making lefse or flatbread

the flour. This was done in good years as well as lean years, and the resulting product was called "barkbread."

Nuts, berries, and herbs were gathered to add to the food supply, and later apples and cherries were raised in Norway. Cows, pigs, sheep, and goats were slaughtered for food, and game such as elk, deer, reindeer, rabbits, and grouse were hunted or trapped; but horse meat was never eaten in those days. Meat and fish were preserved by drying, smoking, salting, or fermenting.

Poultry and eggs were not commonly used by the rural people of Norway, but rather by officials and the upper classes who lived mostly in towns. For a festive occasion, the ordinary people might use a few eggs, a little wheat flour, and perhaps even some sugar to prepare special cakes or bread; but this was not routinely done.

Salt was about the only food product which had to be purchased for use on the farm in Norway. Sugar also could be purchased, but it was not necessary and was seldom used.

Lighting indoors was provided by candles made from animal tallow and a wick, and also by the fireplace. The corner fireplace was where cooking was done in heavy iron pots and copper kettles. Food was served in wooden bowls with wooden spoons made by the men during Norway's long, dark winters. Norwegian peasants did not commonly use the table fork until after 1860 – using bread, the knife, wooden spoons, and also fingers instead. In early times it was common for the entire family to eat from a large bowl or kettle, with little attention paid to sanitary habits. Eating utensils were wiped on the sleeves or an apron before putting them in a rack or in a drawer until the next time they were to be used.

Brewing ale or beer required special talents, not least of which was making the malt. This job was reserved for the master of the house, each generation learning from the previous one, after years of experience in perfecting the pro-

Ale Bowl
Vesterheim Norwegian-American Museum, Decorah, IA

cess. Some of the best barley was placed in a large wooden container and covered with water. There it stood for several days and was stirred occasionally. The best time to make malt was in the summer when it was easiest to get the barley to sprout. Once the malting was successfully completed, this was followed by mashing, boiling and hopping, fermenting, and at last, finishing.

William Williams' description of the beer is rather vivid:

Drinking Horn

"The ale is a turbid liquid of reddish-green color and from its flavor appears to be an infusion of hay, flavored with a bitter decoction of pine knots. The ale made from malt and hops on the other side of the mountain is much better."

On another encounter with Norwegian ale, he said it was *"turbid and green, like the water of an ill-conditioned aquarium."*

This drinking horn above was made by a farmer in Valdres from an ordinary cow's horn. Today its function is entirely decorative, but at one time it was actually a drinking utensil. Drinking horns have been used for ceremonies and rituals for thousands of years in Norway.

Clothing

To find out about clothing worn by Norwegians before the introduction of photography, one must rely on drawings and paintings, descriptions of garments contained in probate records, and the recorded observations of foreign travelers. Clothing design varied from one district to another, but within each area, a distinctive style prevailed which was closely adhered to by the residents of that area. Tradition and utility were two of the most important considerations in the design of Norwegian peasants' clothing.

Clothing worn by the rural population was most commonly made of sturdy wool or linen cloth that had been spun, dyed, and woven at home. Men wore black or gray woolen coats and trousers, often with the addition of a red cap, resembling a nightcap. Stockings were hand-knit at home and shoes were made by a shoemaker at the farm, using wood and leather produced and processed there. Women and children in rural areas wore shoes of similar construction to those used by men and boys.

In her book, *Unprotected Females in Norway*, published in 1857, Emily Lowe records her observation of a woman's attire:

"A white garment was fulled at the neck, a dark-blue cloth of the same shape covered it, having straps which passed over the shoulders; the white being worn alone in summer, when the women were at work, and it was these garments in which the girls were working in the fields. Upon her head she had put a red high cap; shoes and stockings completed her whole clothing; these latter they always have, never going about barefooted in any part of Norway, except near Drammen."

The observations of a British traveler in Norway, Frederick Metcalfe, were published in 1858, in his book, The *Oxonian in Telemarken*:

"Most of the men wore short seamen's jackets, though a few old peasants adhered to the antique green coat of singular cut, while their gray locks, which were parted in the centre of the forehead, streamed patriarchally over their shoulders, shading their strongly-marked countenances. The female side was really very picturesque. The head-dress is a white kerchief, elaborately crimped or plated, but by some ingenious contrivance shaped in front somewhat like the ladies' small bonnets of the present day, with one corner falling gracefully down behind, … Another part of this complicated piece of linen, which is not plated, covers the forehead like a frontlet, almost close down to the eyebrows, so that at a distance they looked just like so many nuns. Nevertheless, they were the married women of the audience. The spinsters' head-dress

was more simple. They wore no cap at all. The back hair, which is braided in two bands or tails with an intermixture of red tape, is brought forward on either side of the head and round the temples just on a level with the front hair. Most of the females wore tight-fitting scarlet bodices edged with green. On either side of their bosom were six silver hooks, to hold a cross chain of the same metal. The snow-white sleeves of the chemise formed a conspicuous feature in the sparkling parterre. One woman wore a different cap from the rest; its upper part was shaped just like a glory, or nimbus; this done by inserting within a light piece of wood of that shape. Her ornaments, too, were not plain silver, but gilt. She was from Strandebarm."

Swaddled baby and ladies at the church gate

The *bunad*, or festive Norwegian folk costume, was made of sturdy fabric and fine workmanship, decorated with embroidery, requiring a great deal of time and a high degree of skill to fashion. There was a costume for men as well as for women. The design of the women's *bunad* was such that it could be let out or taken in, depending on the volume of the wearer, so that the *bunad* which was first worn by a young girl when she was confirmed, was the same as the one she continued to wear on special occasions for the rest of her life. It was worn on special occasions such as baptisms, confirmations, weddings, and

Christmas. Everyday clothing was of plain design, but equally as sturdy as the *bunad*.

The *bunad* as we know it today is a product of the early 20th century and was not what our forefathers commonly wore when they lived in Norway. Each district in Norway has developed its own distinctive costume or *bunad,* based on styles and designs of clothing most commonly worn in a particular district in earlier times.

It was interesting to learn how babies were diapered at a time when laundry facilities were less than ideal. In the Valdres valley babies were swaddled, or wound with a cloth. The first garment was a sort of wrap-around shirt that reached to their thighs. Over that was a red jacket which was somewhat shorter and had ties in the front or back. Next, there were several strips of cloth. First was a strip about 18 inches long and 6 inches wide which was wound over the lower back. Next was a binding about 12" by 6", and then a third strip which was just a little bigger. The fourth strip was about 24" long and was wrapped at an angle from the underarms downward over the toes. Over this was an outer wrapping of thick half-wool woven fabric which was also wound diagonally over the toes. The last strip was an outer wrapping 4 to 6 feet long and 6 inches wide and was all wool. When the baby was wet it had to be unbound and rewrapped with dry clothes. It was necessary to do this about four times a day. Old people in Valdres said that swaddling kept the baby warm and was good for their feet, as the binding kept them straight. When babies got big enough so that they could kick off the bindings, they were put in short dresses. Underneath they wore bindings that could easily be changed when wet. Boys wore dresses until they were 3 to 5 years old, after which they wore pants.

Although I found no detailed account of how diapers were laundered, they most certainly were washed more often than the regular household laundry was done. Laundry day on the farm occurred at rather infrequent intervals; only 3 to 6 times each year—and never in the middle of winter! Customary times for doing laundry were in early spring, in mid-summer, after the fall harvest, and again just before Christmas.

Clothing and household linens were washed in the cookhouse. This is the same building used for brewing and baking, as well as making soap. Throughout the year the housewife saved left-over fat, and when soap-making time came, this was mixed with water, lye, and other ingredients in a large kettle. The mixture was cooked and stirred for several hours. When the housewife decided the soap was ready, it was taken off the fire and left to cool in a flat container. It was cut into pieces for use in the laundry as well as for other household purposes.

Washing Clothes in Hardanger
Vesterheim Norwegian-American Museum, Decorah, IA

After scrubbing the clothes on a washboard in the washtub, white linens were often boiled. After everything was thoroughly rinsed in cold water from a nearby lake, river, or stream, the wash was put outside to dry. Fences were draped with clothing, and white linens were spread on the grass to bleach in the sun. In spite of the fact that laundry was heavy work, it appears that it was women's work — and rarely mentioned in accounts of work on the Norwegian farm.

Writers seldom elaborated on women's work or their position in the old society of rural Norway; however, Samuel Laing compares them with women in England:

> *"The state of manners in this country may appear inconsistent with the statements of other travelers, representing females, even in the highest classes, as holding a lower position in society than in other parts of Europe. ....they do much work, which with us, in any class of society above the lowest would be considered servant's drudgery, such as not sitting down at entertainments, but waiting on the guests; and one lively traveler in Norway, Derwent Conway, reckons the life of a Norwegian lady of rank, little better than that of an English chambermaid. If we inspect the arrangements in Norway with regard to property, this apparent inconsistency will disappear; and the female sex will be found to have in fact more to do with the real business of life, and with those concerns which require mental exertion and talent, than women of the same class in England.*
>
> *... females hold a just position in society, have the influence and participation in its affairs which develop their mental powers, and place them as intelligent beings in a suitable relation to the other sex. If one considers how little of the real business of life in Britain is ever understood by the females of any family above the middle class, the advantage, as intelligent beings having business and duties to perform, is clearly on the side of the Norwegian females."*

In most countries, a woman's place was in the home; but in Norway, a woman's place was wherever she was needed. Early recognition of women's capabilities led to the organization of the Norwegian Society for Women's Rights in 1884. By 1901, women of certain income groups had won the right to vote in local elections, and by

1907 this was extended to national elections. Political equality between men and women was established in 1913 when Norway became one of the first countries in the world to have complete woman suffrage under the law.

Chapter 5

THE CHURCH IN NORWAY

Christianity

Prior to the introduction of Christianity, barely 1000 years ago, Norwegians held pagan beliefs and followed pagan practices, many of them violent. Blood revenge was often carried out to preserve one's honor, humans were sacrificed, and slaves were held. However, at the same time loyalty, hospitality, courage, and faithfulness were required of the Norsemen. The first exposure to Christianity was experienced by Vikings in their plundering raids on monasteries, churches, and cities to the south and west. Attempts at Christianizing Norway were made by missionaries from the south and west; but it was King Olav Haraldsson, who later became St. Olav, who is credited with establishing Christianity in Norway.

King Olav Haraldsson supplied priests and bishops, built churches, and forced people to accept Christianity under the pain of death. In some areas people resisted

Voss Church. In 1271 a letter from King Magnus Lagabøte encouraged Voss parishioners to replace the wooden church with this stone church. It was completed in 1277. *Vesterheim Norwegian-American Museum, Decorah, IA.*

Christianity, resulting in priests being killed and churches burned. It took almost a century of local missionary efforts to firmly establish Christianity throughout the country. Churches were organized according to local conditions and needs, and church laws became a part of Norwegian law. The result was a national folk church that became the single most influential institution in rural Norway and remained so for centuries.

With the introduction of Christianity, the common people experienced an improvement in their status. No longer were they mere chattel whose function was to serve their superiors but were recognized as human beings with souls. Spiritual discipline and religious instruction were required of everyone, regardless of their social status. The first requirement was for everyone over the age of 15 to learn by rote from the priest the creed, the Lord's Prayer, and the Ave Maria. By the early 12th century most populated areas had a priest and a place of worship, but it was not until 1153 that Norway became an independent church province of the Roman Catholic Church. One hundred and fifty years later Norway had 2,000 priests, 28 monasteries and convents, and 1,300 churches. Cathedrals, as well as several hundred churches, were made of stone, but about 800 churches were the familiar wood *stav* churches. These buildings were richly decorated with dragon heads, crosses, and other ornamentation.

Not only the church but the entire country was devastated by the bubonic plague (Black Death) which swept across Norway in the middle of the 14th century. Approximately one-half of the general population was wiped out, and about 80% of the clergy. Large areas of the country were totally deserted, and farm buildings and churches were left to decay.

The Lutheran Church

On September 2, 1537, King Christian III signed the Danish Church Ordinance establishing the Lutheran Church in Denmark. The previous year Norway had been declared a province of Denmark; thus the ordinance of 1537 was mandatory for Norway also. King Christian sent his representatives to Norway where the ordinance was officially approved in June 1539, and the king's commissioners took control of all church property. Convents, monasteries, bishop's estates, and all properties of the church were confiscated by the Crown. Priests were ordered to become Lutheran or leave their parishes. Those refusing to do so were ousted and ordered to leave the country, never to return. Those who chose to stay in their parishes were required to learn a new order of service, which was little more than an abridged version of the Roman Catholic Mass.

The process of establishing Lutheranism, as well as building new churches, was a slow one. It took a generation to train pastors to fill the pulpits, and still another generation before the laity had fully accepted the new religion. The new religion was perceived as just another inconvenience thrust upon the people of Norway by their king in Denmark. Most bishops and pastors came from Denmark, so it was natural that the Norwegians had feelings of resentment toward them. A rather derisive attitude toward these "foreigners" is evident in Norway's folk tales. Some of those stories depict the local sexton, who is Norwegian and of far lower status, to be much more clever than the Danish *prest* (pastor). With the founding of the University of Christiania (Oslo) in 1811, Norway was able to train her own clergy. Subsequently, respect for the profession increased, and Norwegian pastors came to be held in high esteem by the masses. They were respected and often perceived as father, doctor, and peacemaker, holding an office in the highest profession in the country.

Church Buildings

Early Norwegian Christians began building churches known as *stav* (stave) churches. According to Håkon Christie, noted Norwegian architectural historian:

> *"The distinguishing feature of a stave church is that it is corner posts (staves) and wall planksstanding on sills. These walls are known as stave walls, hence the name stave church."*

Progress in church-building was slow and complicated by setbacks in Christianity's advance, but eventually, many churches were built.

By the early 1800s, there were about 1,300 churches in Norway, of which 320 were *stav* churches. Norway had become a Christian nation, yet the churches carried remnants of paganism, as well as Christian symbols, in their design and ornamentation.

Church construction in Norway came to a halt in the 14th century following the Black Death and did not resume until after the Reformation. With the Reformation came the construction of new churches. Some of the old *stav* churches were remodeled and enlarged and continued to be used, but many more had fallen into ruin and were torn down. Many of the little brown wooden churches were replaced with larger and lighter churches so that by 1800 less than 100 *stav* churches remained. Additional church construction was made necessary by a law that was passed in 1851, requiring all churches to be large enough to hold 60% of the congregation. In some areas, the existing churches, including *stav* churches, were torn down and replaced. Of the 100 *stav* churches that survived until 1800, only 30 are standing today. Twenty-nine remain in Norway, but one was sold to the King of Prussia in 1840. He had it taken down and rebuilt in Silesia (now Poland) where it still stands.

A law was passed in 1735 which made church attendance compulsory. In 1736 another law was enacted which made confirmation in the State Church of Norway compulsory. Church attendance was further strengthened in the 1790s by the lay revival movement within the existing Lutheran Church led by Hans Nielsen Hauge. He was the famous Norwegian lay evangelist responsible for the spiritual awakening of Norwegians in the first part of the 1800s. Hauge stressed emancipation of the laity from the clergy and ruling class and encouraged members to take a more active role in the church. The combined effect of the above influences served to increase church attendance and encouraged remodeling of old churches and the building of new ones.

Up until the time of the Reformation all church property was held by the church in Rome, but with the establishment of Lutheranism, church property became the property of the Danish Crown. Along with ownership of churches and monasteries came the added responsibility of maintenance. At the end of the Great Northern War in 1720, Denmark's treasury was so badly depleted that it was impossible to keep church buildings in the hands of the crown. In an effort to replenish her empty coffers, Denmark sold churches and church property in Norway to wealthy families. Many of these churches remained in private hands until the last half of the 19th century.

The Urnes Stav Church

The Urnes Stav Church is of special interest in our family and "Urness" is the surname used by this branch of my family. Urnes Stav Church is located in Urnes on a small peninsula in Luster on the Sognefjord. This is the home church of my paternal great grandparents who emigrated from Hafslo, Norway in 1857. It is the oldest remaining *stav* church in Norway. Surveys using dendrochronology, a measurement based on a tree's growth rings, show that the logs used to build this church were felled in the winter of 1131-1132. This was the fourth and final church built on the site.

Urnes Stav Church
Photo by G. Rohlfing

Elements of wood carvings and other ornaments inside and outside of the church were preserved from previous churches. Dendrochronology reveals that the oldest timber logs found among those in the Urnes church were growing in AD 765. Photodendrometry was used to determine the date of the wood used for the famous wood carving on the north side of the church. They found that that particular piece dates back to 1070 which would be proof that it was saved and reused from the previous church. The unique carving features asym-

Model of Urnes Stav Church   Urnes Stav Church front door

metrical, graceful, intertwined lines, slender animals with almond-shaped eyes, and spirals to designate hip joints. The "Urnes style" was named after this north portal and is considered the last period of Viking Art between the 8th and the 11th centuries. Through the ages and into the 21st century artists have been inspired by the artistic fundamentals used to create works of art in the "Urnes style" through wood carvings, jewelry, clipart, paintings, and more.

The Urnes Style

The Urnes style has been replicated in metal, jewelry, and wood over the past 900 years. The wood carving on the left is the original from 1070. The wood carving on the right by Don Rorvik of Wisconsin was commissioned by the author. It is a replica in the Urnes-style portal carving on the north wall of the present Urnes church, Norway's oldest *stav* church built in the 11th century, exactly like the original.

Left:
Carving from Urnes
church 1070

Right:
Carving by Don Rorvig
21st Century

Brooches belonging to family members

Urnes Door Crown carved by
Becky Lusk

North portal of Urnes
Church

Norway's 50 øre
coin depicting the
Urnes beast

Serving Board carving
by Becky Lusk

The Clergy

The state church of Norway was divided into five bishoprics, each with its own bishop. These were further divided into deaneries, made up of several adjoining parishes and supervised by a dean or Probst. It was the responsibility of the dean to oversee 5 or 6 parishes. They supervised the state of church property and buildings, and also the performance of parish pastors. Each parish was made up of a head church and several annex churches, under the charge of a single pastor. In some parishes, the pastor was assisted by a *kapellan* or *medhjelper*. The *kapellan* was usually a young ordained minister who acted as an apprentice to the pastor. The *medhjelper* was a layperson who was an assistant to the pastor.

Bishop Jakob von der Lippe 1797-1878
Vesterheim Norwegian-American Museum, Decorah, IA

In rural Norway, the pastor lived on the *prestegård* (pastor's farm) which was provided by the government. A place on this farm was appropriated for the wife of the pastor in the event that she became a widow. In addition to the pastor's place, several other farms belonging to the church provided a small additional income to the pastor's farm. The rent on these places was paid in goods and services provided for the pastor's household. A formal contract, which was reviewed about every 5 years, clearly defined the renters' obligations.

It was not until the establishment of the University in Christiania (Oslo) in 1811, that it was possible for clergymen to be educated in Norway. Until Denmark lost control of Norway in 1814, most church leaders in Norway were Danish and received their clerical training in Denmark or Germany.

Clergymen were government officials and were paid in money and goods. In addition to a set monetary payment, they received a certain portion of goods from each church member, as well as special voluntary offerings. These offerings were usually placed on the altar at Christmas and Easter. As members of the congregation filed around the altar, the pastor knelt in a state of reverence. In addition to salary and special offerings, the pastor's income was supplemented by special fees which he received for performing baptisms, confirmations, weddings, and funerals. In *Journal of a Residence in Norway*, published in the 1830s, Laing tells about the salary of clergymen:

> *"The incomes of the clergy run, in country parishes, from 800 to 1600 dollars. 800 dollars is sufficient for a family living in the best way according to the fashion of the country, and in its best society. In Bergen, Christiania, and other towns, there are, of course, large incomes, and a more expensive scale of living; but the towns are too small, and the large incomes acquired in commercial or professional pursuits too rare, to have such influence upon society as in England, and the division among the children necessarily makes frugality and moderation the prevailing principles of living.*
>
> *The incomes of the country clergy are derived from a small modus or payment of grain, in lieu of tithe, from each farm. Tithe of fish is paid in Finnmark and Nordland, and some parts of Bergen Amt, as there is no other produce. But a tithe of agricultural produce is commuted into a payment of grain, not reckoned burdensome, as it is not above two or three bushels for the largest farm, yet, from the great number of farms in a parish, it makes a considerable income.*
>
> *A third source of income is from Easter and Christmas offerings, and pretty high offerings or due for marriages, christenings, and funerals. The public functionaries and the clergy have also comparatively considerable incomes; but in no respect do their houses, either inside or outside, or*

their entertainments, depart from the ordinary style of the country..... The clergy are, in political rights and privileges, on the same footing as any other class of the community."

Even though the clergy received far higher incomes than others, they were not granted special privileges.

The economy of Norway varied from district to district, as well as from year to year. According to some authorities, the annual salary of a pastor in the first half of the 1800s was about 500 dollars, considerably less than what Laing states. However, the parish in which he resided was near Trondheim and was perhaps one of the more affluent ones at that time.

The *Klokker*

Next to the pastor, the most important religious leader in the community was the *klokker* (sexton or precentor), who might also be the local school teacher. At one time the sexton was required to serve several congregations, but by the early 1800s, each congregation was to have its own sexton. The most capable young man in the community was chosen by the pastor to be trained for this position. Sometimes they were trained entirely by the pastor while at other times they were sent away to the nearest city where there was a Latin School. The sexton's main responsibility was to lead the singing, ring the church bell, and read scripture for church services. Those who were also teachers were responsible for preparing young people for confirmation in the state church of Norway.

The *klokker* lived on the *klokkergård* (sexton's farm), which was often a small place on a larger farm. Although his position was one of honor, his salary was poor. There is a saying that translates: "When it rains on the pastor, it drips on the sexton." In the early 1800s, a sexton in Sogn received an annual income of six dollars, plus 12 bushels of barley. In addition, he received 12 dollars for his service as a school teacher. He also had a little extra income, but the source of that is not mentioned. Although the sexton was far beneath the pastor in income as well as social status, he was highly respected in the community.

The Sabbath

Samuel Laing writes about the Sabbath:

"The evening of Saturday and the morning of Sunday make the seventh day, or Sabbath, according to the Lutheran Church. This interpretation is so fully established, and interwoven with their thinking and acting, that entertainments, dances, card parties, and all public amusements, take place regularly on Sunday evenings."

Services were held at one parish church each Sunday, and on other Sundays, devotions were held in the homes. The church was the social center of the community, and the motive for attending church services was not limited to religious ardor.

The time before and after services were used for secular purposes. The churchyard was a place where people gathered on a regular basis to learn the news of the community, meet friends and relatives, conduct business, settle accounts, read public notices and carry on other necessary activities. *Recollections of a Residence in Norway* (author unknown) published about 1860 tells:

"Although it is the great day for transacting business in the country after divine service, yet in other respects the Norwegians observe it as one of rest. Their sabbath commences at 4 p.m. on Saturday afternoon, and no dancing or public amusement are allowed that night. All bills are commonly paid and accounts are settled on Sunday, ... I am speaking of the country, where their excuse is that there is often no chance of seeing each other during the week, people living so far apart."

The pastor appeared at the church in his black robe and white ruff to conduct

Urnes Stav Church altar

church services on Sunday morning. He was assisted by the sexton, who read parts of the service and led the singing. Music was an important part of the worship service. If there was an organ in the church, an organist's services were required, but often there was no organ, and the sexton led the singing unaccompanied. With the women seated on one side of the church and the men on the other, the service proceeded with hymn singing, reading of the Collect, Epistle, and the Gospel, followed by a very long sermon. It appears that men and women of the upper-class families were permitted to

Dale Church pulpit in Luster

sit together in special pews located at the front of the church, and often elevated to the level with the chancel dais, but the mingling of sexes among the "common folk" was not permitted in the church.

Gudstjenester (divine services) were solemn, orderly, and dignified when conducted by a capable pastor, which was usually the case; however, there were exceptions. In Jon Laberg's book, *Hafslo*, published in 1926, he tells of a visit by the Dean of Inner Sogn to the Hafslo parish in 1830. Church services were to begin at 11 o'clock, but few people were there, and almost none of the young people who were preparing for confirmation had arrived. Finally, the service began, but by then babies were crying and small children were making noise. The dogs that had followed their masters to the church were barking and fighting in the churchyard, so when the church door was opened there was such a din that it was difficult to hear the pastor. When weddings were held in the church, guns were shot and fiddles played in the churchyard. The Dean ordered a stop to this disrespectful practice.

On a visit to the Hafslo parish in 1834, the Dean reported that there continued to be much disorder and depravity, and conditions were generally in utter ruin. Morals of the young people were especially bad, the cause of which was the rampant use of hard liquor. He blamed the innkeeper in part, and also those who loaned out their houses for debauched gatherings.

In 1858 the local pastor in Hafslo complained of the lack of morals and manners exhibited by the common people, although he admitted that there were some exceptions to this bad behavior. Weddings and funerals lasted for four or five days with an abundance of hard liquor. According to the pastor, young people were a wild bunch, and "night courting" was still going on, especially in the fall.

While conditions in some parishes seemed out of control at times, more appropriate behavior prevailed in most churches, and a solemn Sunday service was conducted with order and dignity. Regardless of conditions in different parishes, even the most inept pastors were required to administer the sacraments and perform the rites mandated by the State Church of Norway. A law was passed in 1688 which required pastors to keep a written record of all baptisms, marriages, burials, and other pastoral duties. Confirmation and Introduction records (for women approximately 6 weeks after they had a baby) began in 1736, but Introduction was dropped in 1814. That same year, smallpox vaccination records, new arrivals in the parish, and transfers out of the parish were added to the records. Some church records begin as early as 1623, but most begin about 1700.

Samuel Laing sums up the State Church of Norway:

> "In principle and doctrine, it is purely Lutheran, as it has never been touched by the hand of power, nor altered by the spirit of innovation, but remains as it was originally moulded after the subversion of popery."

Baptism

If a newly married couple had not already had their first child and had it christened before the marriage ceremony took place, the possibilities of having a child christened in the next year were good.

The baby was carried to the church in its proper christening robes, where the sexton put water in a bowl, and the pastor performed the ceremony.

In *The Oxonian in Telemarken*, by Fredrick Metcalfe, published in 1858, he describes the baptism of an infant:

Baptismal font from Hedal Church
Photo by G. Rohlfing

"Very small and very red babies, not many hours old, I believe — such is the almost superstitious eagerness with which these good folk rush to have that sacred rite administered — were now brought to be christened. No font was visible; there was, however, an angel suspended by a cord from the roof, with deep, flesh-colored legs and arms, and a gilt robe. In its right hand was a bowl, in its left a book. The clerk, a little man in a blue sailor's jacket, here dispatched a girl for some water, which was brought, and poured into the bowl, and the ceremony proceeded; which being concluded, the angel was pulled up again midway to the ceiling."

Metcalfe added the following footnote:

"Ström, in his description of Söndmöre, relates that in the hard winter of 1755, of thirty children born in the parish of Volden not one lived, solely because they were brought to the church directly after they were born, but even in the present day in the register books notices may be found, such as 'died from being brought too early to church.'"

From the church records in the Norwegian Archives, one learns that babies were, indeed, very young when brought to the church for baptism. At one time the church had a rule that babies should be baptized by the time they were 8 days old. This was not an enforceable rule as pastors served several congregations, and services were not held in every church on a weekly basis. If there was a danger that the baby might die, the baby's father or a neighbor baptized the infant at home, and the rite was repeated later at church by the pastor. Usually, the baby was baptized the first time the pastor held services in the local congregation following the baby's birth and seldom was the child more than a few weeks old.

Sponsors at baptism were usually close relatives, but occasionally they were highly respected neighbors. Following the baptism ceremony, large groups of close relatives and friends gathered to celebrate, each providing food to the extent to which they could afford it.

In the 1800s the rate of infant mortality was high in Norway, as it was in all countries at that time. Hygienic standards during delivery were very poor, and the death of the mother and/or child in childbirth was a feared and common fate. Frequent pregnancies, as well as deliveries under unhygienic conditions in cold and drafty houses, weakened the resistance of both mother and child. Many infants died before reaching two years of age. Family planning, apart from believing that nursing gave a certain amount of protection from becoming pregnant, was unknown.

Norway's first educated midwife came to Trondheim in 1753, but it was well into the 1800s before it became common to have the services of a trained midwife at the birth of the baby. In country districts babies were born at home with an untrained *jordmor* (midwife) in attendance, assisted by one or more women in the district. Their only training was from experience, combined with information and advice, which had been passed from one woman to another, and from one generation to the next.

It was an old tradition to celebrate the successful delivery of a baby. Women from the neighborhood brought "bedfood" – usually porridge – for the bedridden housewife. Little emphasis was given to the actual birth date, and individual birthdays were not celebrated, but the date of baptism was the date to be remembered.

Until about 1814, mothers were required to take part in a rite of purification following childbirth. The rite was called "Introduction," and was based on Old Testament teachings. Women were considered unclean and needed to be purified in a religious ceremony before being accepted back into the congregation. The rite usually took place about six weeks after giving birth.

Vaccination

Another important day in the life of young children in Norway, and a rather unique dress-up occasion, was when the appointed government official arrived in the neighborhood to administer smallpox vaccination.

Smallpox vaccination was introduced in Norway by the clergy in the 1780s. In the beginning, pastors did the vaccinating themselves, vaccinating their own children first to demonstrate to the peasant population that it was a safe procedure. Once the practice was accepted, a midwife, the sexton, or another resident of the community, was taught to vaccinate children. A Royal Order was issued by the King of Norway and Denmark in 1810, requiring everyone to have a certificate of vaccination. As the postal system in Norway was expensive and unreliable prior to 1805, it is almost certain that the time and place for vaccination was announced at church services. Once a year the government representative in charge of smallpox immunization arrived in the community. Mothers and children appeared in their best attire at the appointed time, making vaccination a social event in the old rural society of Norway. Metcalfe describes vaccination day in Hardanger:

> "We overtook a number of women, dressed in their best. The inventory is as follows: A lily-white, curiously plated head-dress, the getting-up of which must take an infinity of time and trouble; red or parti-coloured bodice, black grown, and stockings of the same colour, cut off at the ankle, while on the foot were white socks with red edging, and shoes with high

leather insteps, such as were worn in the days of the cavaliers. By their side were a lot of children, also in their best attire.

Where are you all going to this fine day?' "It's vaccination day, and we are all going to meet the doctor, who will be here from Strandebarm by two o'clock. We must all of us get a bolen-attest (certificate of vaccination). That's the King's order."

Vaccination Certification from mid-1800s
Vesterheim Norwegian-American Museum, Decorah, IA

Vaccinations were recorded in a special section of the church book. It showed the father's name, child's name, baptism date, age, vaccination date, and name of the person administering the vaccination. Church records seem an unlikely place to record vaccination, yet several factors make it the most logical place. Following the order of 1810 regarding vaccination, the church refused to confirm or marry those who could not certify that they had been vaccinated. With vaccination records in the church book, the pastor could easily verify the qualifications of candidates for these rites. Another important factor in recording vaccination in the church record is that few people in the old rural society of Norway were able to write. Prior to the 1860s, the pastor was one of the few, if not the only person, in a rural district with that skill.

Confirmation

The rite of confirmation in the Lutheran faith was one of the most important events in a young Norwegian's life. After successfully completing their study of Luther's Catechism and the Bible, young people, usually 14 or 15 years old, were confirmed. Once each year those who were ready for confirmation were lined up on either side of the church aisle on a given Sunday and examined orally. This rite is described by Samuel Laing:

> "There is here a strict examination by the bishop, or the Probst, or rural dean, into the young person's knowledge of his moral and religious duties, his capacity, acquirements, and character; and it is only after a long previous preparation by this parish minister, equal almost to a course of education, the confirmants being instructed singly as well as in classes, that one individual is presented for this examination. I was present lately at confirmation of about twenty young persons in our parish church by the Probst. The examination, in presence of the congregation, occupied nearly two hours. .....
> To pass such a confirmation implies that the young person is well-grounded in the principles of his moral and religious duties and is of good character and understanding.
>
> In the face of the congregation, the confirmant has shown that he can read and has the use of his mental faculties to an ordinary degree, according to his station, and has moral and religious principles to direct him."

Following the rite of confirmation young people became members of the state church, a condition fixed by law. At that time, they were considered adults, and ready to support themselves. Without religious confirmation, a person could not hold public office, receive any kind of license, or receive the protection of the law.

Burial

When a death occurred, the minister or an official in charge of the burial was notified. Immediately after death, the straw was removed from the mattress upon which the deceased was resting when he died. The straw was taken outside and burned. The corpse was taken to an out-building on the farm while family members sang a hymn. It was usually an old woman in the neighborhood who was in charge of preparing the corpse for burial. She propped up the chin, closed the eyes, and if it was a man, shaved it. After the body was bathed and dressed it was placed in a coffin with the arms folded over the chest. Sometimes a man made his own wooden coffin, but more often it was the neighborhood carpenter who made it and blackened it with *kjønrøk* (lamp black.)

Word of death in the community sometimes traveled slowly, so it was often several weeks before the funeral could be held, especially in winter. The time between death and burial was considerably shorter in summer, yet several days were necessary to prepare for a proper funeral celebration, sometimes referred to as a *gravøl*. Baking, brewing, and butchering were required to prepare food for all who came and stayed for several days. A special beer, also called *gravøl* (burial beer), was brewed for the *gravfest* (burial festival). Relatives and neighbors brought special food to the home of the deceased.

When all was properly prepared, the coffin was carried into the house. Two candles were placed on a table at the head, and a hymnal was placed on the deceased's chest. After everyone had viewed the corpse, a meal was served at the home. The funeral service began with a *kjøgemester* (master of ceremonies) conducting a short service at the home. A hymn was sung while the body was carried outside and taken to the church for burial. It was placed on a wagon or sled, depending on the season; but where the terrain was steep and the path very narrow, it was often necessary to tie the coffin between two horses, one in front of the other, and carry it to the church in that manner.

The procession of relatives and friends in carriages or sleds, and those on foot, went at a solemn pace to the church, singing hymns along the way. When the procession came within sight of the church, the church bell began to toll and continued until all in the procession were gathered around the place of burial. To the singing of hymns and reading of appropriate scripture, the burial took place, following which those who had dug the grave completed the burial. Often the minister was not present for burial, but on his next visit to the church would throw a handful of dirt on the new grave in the cemetery as he read the formal committal service.

The ceremony was located in the churchyard. Due to the lack of tillable land in Norway, vast areas were not set aside for cemeteries, so the same plot was reused for another burial after an interval of 20 or 30 years. Small wooden markers marked the graves, stating only the name, age, and date of the birth and death of the deceased. No epitaph was used – perhaps due to the lack of pretense in the Norwegian people – as most often the epitaph states what the deceased should have been, not what he was. Following the burial, it was a considerably livelier procession that made its way back to the deceased's home. Much food and drink had been prepared which awaited the mourners. Several days of feasting and visiting took place before everyone returned to their homes following the funeral celebration.

Chapter 6

COURTING AND MARRIAGE

I t is said that in olden times in Norway a bachelor was unknown and an impossibility. Not only did a man need a wife to bear children who would then grow up to help with work on the farm, but he also needed a wife to prepare food, spin, weave, knit, sew clothes, milk the cows and goats, shear the sheep, churn the butter, make cheese, bake, brew, help make hay, and perform other sundry duties. Most people married and rarely was the marriage broken except by death. Life became extremely difficult, if not impossible, without a mate; so when disease or childbirth claimed a spouse, the survivor was quick to find a replacement.

The process of selecting a mate in Norway in the 19th century, and earlier, followed certain patterns of behavior. Economic and social conditions of the time played a considerable role in the secular aspects of courtship and marriage customs, while church tradition regulated the religious formalities.

The sphere of courting activity was rather limited during the early 1800s, therefore young men usually chose their mates from within the community where they lived. Parents sometimes played a role in the selection of mates for their children, but it was often left up to the young person to make the final choice. Young people met in school, in confirmation class, at weddings, at funerals, and at social gatherings in the community. Another place where romances were known to blossom was at the mountain farm during the summer. Young girls went with the cows and goats to spend the summer there, working as dairymaids. On weekends, the young men who stayed at the main farm would go to visit the girls in the mountains. Many marriages resulted from those visits under Norway's midnight sun.

Drawing of preparations for a new bride by Adolf Tidemand 1857
Vesterheim Norwegian-American Museum, Decorah, IA

Another method of courtship was called "night courting," whereby boys who were free to go visiting at night went in groups, or alone, to visit girls. The girl who was expecting a visitor would lie fully clothed in her bed, and the boy would visit her there. Sometimes he would be invited to take off his jacket and shoes, and even lie under the covers - maybe for the entire night. This is sometimes referred to as "bundling," an acceptable practice in the old agrarian society of Norway. Even the early followers of Hans Nielsen Hauge's pietistic teachings accepted this means of courtship. Night courting was about the only way for boys and girls to mingle, for at church, as well as other social gatherings, boys and girls sat in separate groups.

When a couple had been courting for some time, the young boys of the area would begin teasing and trying to disturb the couple when they were together. This was called "jingling" or "belling" the couple. It was carried out by rattling cowbells or kettles filled with stones. Any couple who was "belled," but did not get married, was liable to be shamed. "Scattering" was another old custom in some districts, among them, Inner Sogn. The custom was to scatter sawdust from the house of the girl to the house of her suitor.

When a couple was ready to be engaged, the marriage proposal was sometimes made through an intermediary or "wooing man," who spoke to the girl's father on behalf of the boy's father. If both parties agreed to the marriage, a binding engagement was made to which both were committed in a betrothal ceremony. In the eyes of the law, this was a distinct status, often of long duration, and was morally and legally the binding contract between a man and woman. According to tradition in Norway, unmarried peasants who were engaged to be married must remain as house servants until a *husmannsplass* (cotter's place) became vacant, at which time the couple could marry. Often a child was born before the ceremony took place; however, subsequent marriage of the parents made the child legitimate.

I found no evidence of engaged girls being punished for having a child before marriage; but if an unattached woman had a child born out of wedlock, she was usually the one scorned, not the child's father. The number of times each parent had "committed fornication" was noted in the baptism records of children born out of wedlock. When punishment was meted out (and that seemed to be rarely), it was usually in the form of humiliation rather than imprisonment and was often more severe for the woman than for the man. In some communities, a girl who had an illegitimate child was placed in irons outside the church on Sunday so that the people coming to services could kick her, hit her, spit on her, abuse her verbally, or otherwise. This was done three Sundays for each offense. The early church books show records of unmarried girls receiving "Public Absolution" in the church following the birth of an illegitimate child.

Frequently the bride was pregnant before she married. This was deemed perfectly proper as long as the couple was betrothed. It also assured the man that he had chosen a mate capable of childbearing and that she could provide him with an heir. Sometimes it was necessary to hurry things up a bit so that the wedding would be over before the midwife had to be summoned, other times the wedding came several months or years after the first baby arrived.

Country Weddings

After the wedding date was set, the prospective groom, or a specially appointed *bedemann* (inviting man), went out to extend an invitation to all the relatives of both bride and groom. The *bedemann* was a person whose function was to deliver invitations to social functions and to arrange weddings and funerals. Included among the invited guests were those who lived in a clearly defined area called the *bearlage* (inviting circle), Everyone who has invited contributed something to the food supply for the wedding celebration. These gifts of food were called *beinings* and were usually delivered to the farm the day before the wedding and stored in the *stabbur* (storehouse). One of the most capable women at the farm was appointed *Mor i buret* and placed in charge of the food. It was most important that she remember who sent what so that the *beinings* from the nearest and most important relatives would occupy a place of honor on the table. Cotters in the area were usually invited to participate in the wedding festivities. Men and boys took care of the horses, harnesses, carriages, carts, etc., and supervised serving the beer. The women and girls took care of serving food to the guests.

It was necessary for marriage banns to be published three times. Should the engagement be broken at any time up to this point, legal procedures, much as the divorce proceedings of our time, were required. Once a marriage had taken place, the bonds were rarely broken. Divorce was possible, but it was considered a disgrace, and far too costly for most people to afford.

Drawing depicting a wedding in the 1850s from Unprotected Females in Norway by Emily Rowe.

It seems that June, October, and early November were popular times for weddings. Not only were these times relatively quiet on the farm, travel conditions were good, and many guests could be conveniently housed when the weather was favorable. Milk, butter, and cheese were in good supply after the dairy animals began producing in the spring, and most plentiful in late summer when the animals and dairymaids returned from the mountain pastures. Following harvest time on the farm, provisions were at their peak, and those involved with the wedding could treat the wedding guests to proper food and drink.

Norwegian Wedding Party in Hardanger around 1900
Vesterheim Norwegian-American Museum, Decorah IA

On the day of the wedding, the *kjøgemester* (master of ceremonies), who was usually the same person as the "inviting man," acted as host, meeting wedding guests as they arrived at the farm, Food was served to everyone before setting out for the church. On the way to the church, the bridal couple was preceded by outriders, fiddlers, and a person with a brandy keg, ready to slake the thirst of anyone in the procession. Next came the bridal couple, followed by the groom's parents, then the bride's parents, close relatives, and finally more distant relatives, friends, and neighbors. The journey to and from the church might go over both land and water. Boats were decorated and processed across the water, much the same as carriages did on land. In Voss, it was traditional for the bride to ride to the church on a decorated horse. Some people were lucky enough to have a horse of their own, but others had to borrow one.

The Sølje

Sølje

The Sølje is a broach traditionally worn by a Norwegian female on her festive *bunad* (folk costume) which is first worn for her confirmation as well as at her wedding. It was designed in such a way that the garment could be altered and used as formal wear for the rest of her life. Americans of Norwegian descent usually do not have the folk costume, but often wear sølje for special occasions.

After the bridal procession entered the church, the bride and groom were seated in wedding chairs at the front of the church. The bride was dressed in the costume of the district, with the addition of a wedding crown, silver jewelry, and ornaments. The crown was made of silver and was highly prized by the family who owned one, and usually passed it on from one generation to the next. In families not owning a wedding crown, one was sometimes available in the district for a small rental fee. Among the poorer folks who could not afford the fee, a crown was improvised of whatever was available, and the bridal couple wore their "best clothing," which was probably quite ordinary.

Unknown artist based on Hans Dahl's *Bridal Party on Sognefjord*
Vesterheim Norwegian-American Museum, Decorah IA

The pastor was present in his black gown with a white ruff at the neck. He conducted the marriage rite according to Norwegian Lutheran Church tradition. The marriage was recorded in the church book, showing the date of marriage, dates when the banns were published, names of bride and bridegroom, parents' names, and witnesses to the marriage, the latter being most often the fathers of the bridal couple.

When the ceremony at the church was over, everyone returned to the farm where the celebration began in earnest – often to last a week or more. It was usually at the groom's home that the wedding was celebrated in early times; however, if the couple was going to live at the bride's farm, that is usually where the celebration took place. Even among the poorer *husmands* folk (cotters) and servants on the farm, some sort of celebration followed the wedding, however humble it may have been. If farmhands and household servants had served at a farm for a considerable time, the farmer might provide for a wedding celebration for them. In addition, he would often present them with a wedding gift of a cow, or a small plot of ground for raising potatoes. Traditional gifts for the couple included breeding

Wedding Spoons
*Vesterheim Norwegian-American
Museum, Decorah IA*

animals, household items, and other things according to what people could afford. Additionally, as a contribution to the newly formed household, it was customary to have "bride money," the placing of money in a bowl by the guests at the wedding.

Metcalfe described a wedding celebration in *The Oxonian in Telemarken*. He had spent the night at a farm near Mobsy in Vest Agder, and in the morning an old lady arrived to borrow the wedding crown from his hostess. She informed him that the wedding procession would pass by on its way from the church at 5 o'clock in the afternoon, so he delayed his departure for Setesdal in order to witness this event. He relates:

"At that hour, the cry of 'They come! They come!' saluted my ears. Down the steep hill leading to the house there came, at a slow pace, first a cariole with the kjøgemester standing on the board behind, holding the reins over the head of the bridesmaid, a fat old lady with a voluminous pile of white upon her head, supposed to be a cap. Next came a cart, containing two spruce young maidens, who wore caps of dark check with broad strings of red satin riband.

Their jackets were of dark blue cloth, and skirt of the same material and colour, with a narrow scarlet edging. Over the jacket was a colored shawl, the ends crossed at the waist, and pinned tight. Add to this a large pink apron, and in their hands a white kerchief. After these came a carriole with four little boys and girls clustered upon it.

But the climax is now reached. The next vehicle, a cart, contains the main actors in the show, the bride and bridegroom, who are people of slender means. He is evidently somewhat the worse, or better, for liquor, and is dressed in the short blue seaman's jacket and trousers, which have become common in Norway wherever the old national costume has disappeared. The bride sat like the image of the goddess Cybele; on her head a turret of pasteboard, covered with red cloth, with flamboyant mouldings of spangles, beads, and gold lace; miserable counterfeit of the fine old Norwegian bridal crown of silver gilt! Nodding over the turret was a plume of manifold feathers mixed with artificial flowers; from behind it streamed a cataract of ribands of some unrelieved by a single lock of hair. She was further dressed in a red skirt with gold belt, a jacket of black brocade, over which was a cuirass (breast plate) of scarlet cloth shining resplendently in front with the national ornament, the Sölje, a circular silver-gilt brooch, three inches in diameter, with some twenty gilded spoon-baits (fishermen will understand what this is) hung on to its rim. Frippery of diverse sorts hung about her person. On each shoulder was an epaulet or bunch of white gauze bows, while the other ends of her arms were adorned by ruffles and white gloves.

As this wonderful procession halted in front of the door, the gallant kjøgemester advanced and lifted the bride in his arms out of the vehicle.

The kjøgemester is a very ancient institution on this occasion. He is the soul of the whole festival. Without him everything would be in disorder or at a stand-still. He is supposed to combine the offices of master of ceremonies, chief butler, speechifier, jester, precentor, and above all, of peacemaker."

Metcalfe noticed there were fiddles providing music for this wedding celebration, and upon inquiring was informed that these observers were "God-fearing people," and would have nothing to do with such vanity. He thought this to be a contradiction, considering the size of the bride, and the difficulty the stalwart master of ceremonies had in lifting her out of the cart. It appeared to Metcalfe that the bride should have married much sooner, as she was quite pregnant!

In addition to the *kjøgemester, Mor i buret* (the official hostess) had a very important position at the wedding celebration. She met the returning wedding party at the door and served as hostess for the next several days of celebrating. She and the *kjøgemester* were in charge, being responsible for placing everyone properly at the table, keeping the crowd entertained, fed, and under control. Singing, dancing, storytelling, eating, and drinking, were the usual activities that occupied the company; however, after consuming much brandy, an occasional fight broke out among the men.

In 1816 the government of Norway removed restrictions on the manufacture of distilled liquor in the home, creating a problem in keeping order at weddings or other gatherings. When *brennevin* (brandy) was freely served and consumed, celebrations often became wild brawls. Minor quarrels, and sometimes violent fights with knives, resulted in severe wounds, sometimes fatal to one or both combatants. In Valdres and Hallingdal, a type of fighting with knives was the means of settling disputes which arose between two brandy-soaked men. Both knives were drawn and each man drove his knife into a wooden bench or door as hard as he could. The part which did not penetrate the wood was bound in such a way as to render that portion of the blade useless, leaving exposed only the part of the blade which had penetrated the wood to drive into the body of his opponent. The two men were strapped together with a belt and began hacking away at each other. Wives and sweethearts were known to go to weddings and Christmas celebrations provided with dressings to bind up the wounds of their men who were often badly mangled, if not killed while fighting in this manner.

In the mid-1800s a law was passed forbidding this type of activity but fighting continued to be a common form of recreation among liquor-saturated Norwegians. It seems that the amiable peace-loving characteristics, generally attributed to these people, disappeared in direct proportion to the increase in the level of alcohol in their blood. However, not all people in Norway abused the use of liquor. Many abstained completely from drinking alcohol and adhered closely to the teaching of the Norwegian Lutheran Church and the pietistic practices advanced by Hans Nielsen Hauge. Some wedding celebrations were simple, sedate affairs; but even among the more pious, lively celebrations were common in rural Norway.

Illegitimacy in Norway

As mentioned in Chapter 2, loose sexual relationships were not uncommon in rural Norway in the old days. It is said that even among the upper classes, including the clergy, the sixth commandment (Thou shall not commit adultery) was often violated. The attitude of the peasants toward illegitimacy varied from one rural community to another. The poet, Henrik Wergeland, reported that in Sogn it was regarded with complete indifference when an unmarried woman had a child. He said that this was not true in Voss, where women who had children out of wedlock were set apart by a special headdress, could not appear on the dance floor at a public dance, and were called "half-wives."

The renowned Eilert Sundt, a researcher of social conditions in Norway, did an extensive study of the character of the people. The results of his research are found in his books which were published in 1857, 1864, and 1866. He reported that for every 100 couples married in Inner Sogn in 1851, 73.5% had illegitimate children. In neighboring Sunnfjord, another district in Sogn, the percentage was 21.8%. According to another source, 53% of the children born in Inner Sogn were illegitimate. Sundt does not mention the binding engagement, or intention to marry, on the part of the couples with so-called "illegitimate" children. It was not unusual for engaged couples to have several children before they married. The children were left with relatives, often the grandparents, while the parents continued to work as servants. Sometimes it was necessary for one or both of the unmarried couple to leave the home community to find work;

but when they were able, they returned home, were married, and established a home together with their children. The children were then considered legitimate.

Sundt accounts for the high rate of illegitimacy in Sogn by the character of the residents, as well as the courting customs of that area. He said that the lively and light-headed Sogn natives were more likely to have a fast love affair than were the more sedate people of Sunnfjord, immediately to the west. Servants in Sogn had almost unbridled freedom, and no civil laws prohibited them from living together, so it was seldom that one would see a servant girl who did not have one or more children. Surprisingly, this did not seem to hinder her prospects for marriage.

When an unmarried traveling man reached a farm in Inner Sogn late at night, he was free to seek lodging in the barn with the servants, often sharing the same bed with the girls there. Many dwellings were so small that there was room for only the parents, the youngest children, and maybe the old grandparents, to sleep in the house. Older children, and servants, of both sexes, shared beds in the barn or other out-buildings. It was not only casual sleeping arrangements that led to illegitimate births; ignorance and indifference were also factors.

Unconventional Marriages

It was difficult, if not impossible, for a widow or widower to manage alone on a farm in Norway during the 18th and 19th centuries. Spouses were often taken by disease, accident, or childbirth. It was not easy to find a replacement because most capable people of a proper age were already married. For that reason, it was necessary to consider the advantages of marriage to those who were available.

If a healthy, young, capable prospect was not available, an older mate, particularly one with some material wealth, was satisfactory. For example, an ugly old widow with many dependent children, but who owned property, had a much brighter prospect for remarriage than an attractive young widow with no property. Few, if any, children would be born to an older wife, so there would be fewer additional mouths to feed; and when the old wife died, the husband could continue to live on his deceased wife's farm as long as he wanted, provided he did not marry again. Similarly, a poor young widow might have to settle for an old man who could provide a home for her and her brood.

While researching this subject, it became apparent that unconventional marriages were rather commonplace. The 1801 census of Norway lists a man who was 49 years old with a wife who was 85. A family account from Sogn tells of a 50-year-old widow with seven children who married a 27-year-old man. The woman was the sexton's widow, so the man's status was elevated in the community when he married her. In another case, a 64-year-old widow married a 28-year-old man.

An example of a stormy marriage was that of a 43-year-old widow whose husband died of leprosy, after which she married an 18-year-old cotter's son with no prospects for ever inheriting property. The woman owned a farm and an inn. The young husband saw this as an opportunity to become not only a farmer but an innkeeper as well. These were rather lofty ambitions for a simple cotter's son at the time. It turned out that he was abusive, a poor manager, and mistreated his stepdaughters, so after 15 years of marriage, his wife divorced him.

Similarly, on the east side of the Lusterfjord lived a 65-year-old widower with 6 children, 13 to 31 years of age, who married a 19-year-old girl. With her, he had 5 more children, the last one born when he was 78-years-old.

It was not unheard of for a couple to have a marriage and baptism the same day. An example of this is the 24-year-old man and 32-year-old woman who appeared at the cathedral in Bergen on April 8, 1832, with their baby girl, 4 weeks old. The pastor married the couple, following which he baptized their baby.

Another couple who had a baby before they were married, emigrated. The unmarried parents and their 1 ½-year-old daughter went to America. It was not until several months after they were settled in one of the immigrant communities of Wisconsin that the couple finally got married.

Conditions of marriage, as demonstrated by the rural population of Norway in the 19th century, simply indicate that people did what seemed appropriate at a given time and place, and should not be judged by current standards.

Chapter 7

EDUCATION IN NORWAY

The arrival of the Reformation in Norway in 1536 precipitated the first actual need for the common people to learn something about religion. With the new faith came a new system of worship, and ordinary folks were expected to participate. The pastor was one of the few educated people in the parish so it fell to him to instruct his flock. This practice became the forerunner of organized education for all people in Norway.

The pastor's teaching efforts began by teaching adults as well as children. Teaching materials were nonexistent, and the few available books were written in Danish or Latin and cost-prohibitive. In order to teach his parishioners, the pastor read from Luther's Catechism, and the people in the congregation repeated it over and over until it was committed to memory. After the first hymn book appeared in Norway in 1569, hymns were taught the same way. Although the hymnal contained only Danish and Latin hymns, the congregation was able to learn them by rote. All books were in Danish, which was written much the same as Norwegian, but the pronunciation was different. If the pastor read in Danish, using the Norwegian pronunciation, his parishioners were able to understand.

The first printing press arrived in Norway in 1643, about a century after the Reformation. For the first time, books written in the Norwegian language were available, but they were very expensive and few people could afford them. The first books were mostly religious books such as the Bible and Luther's Catechism, as well as hymn books and devotional books. Few people were able to read, so only the pastor, and a few others who could afford them, owned books. Even after people in the rural districts learned to read, economics prevented most of them from purchasing books. As late as 1788 only 5 people in Hafslo, a parish of about 2000 people, owned Bibles. An estate was settled in the same parish of Inner Sogn in 1806, and among the deceased's possessions were 3 books: a book of sermons, a hymn book, and a travel book.

From very early in Norway's history, schools were maintained for the children, especially sons of clergymen and government officials, most of them of Danish background. Promising students in parishes of Norway were chosen by the pastor to attend teacher training schools. These were called Cathedral Schools and provided training for boys who would later become pastors. They were located in the large towns, and later became known as Latin Schools. When school was not in session the boys traveled throughout country districts as missionaries, telling stories, singing, preaching, and also begging. For their efforts, they received monetary contributions, food, and large quantities of drink. According to Karen Larsen's *A History of Norway*, the activities on the boys' missionary journeys were not all virtuous and often had a detrimental effect on the boys' morals and manners.

It was the law of 1736, legally establishing Confirmation in the Lutheran Church, which led to organized education for all children. Norway enacted a school law in 1739 which provided for a system of elementary schools financed by a general tax. The law itself was well-intended, but it was not possible to provide a quality education for everyone when there were no schools to train teachers. When control of the schools became the responsibility of the church parish in 1741, it became the duty of the parish pastor to secure teaching candidates and train them. The Bergen-based publication, *Tourist Magazine*, No. 1, 1991, tells about the School Law of 1739 and early education:

> "The school master must speak to the children in decent and honorable language. He must not speak to anyone contemptuously, because no matter how common or poor they may be, they are still plants of the Lord. He must not strike anyone with a stick or hand, nor administer blows to the head or act in any other rough manner.

"The clergy, who were the only people who could read, would have preferred a permanent school, linked to a schoolhouse – that would have given them an opportunity to provide more instruction, they felt. The farmers wanted a traveling school, i.e. instruction would be given for a couple of weeks in the home of one of the farmers, and then for a couple of weeks in another home. That way, they saved on the expense of a school building."

It was not only the financial burden of maintaining a school building that concerned the Norwegian farmers, but it was also the inconvenience of a permanent school. Children, even the very young ones, were often needed at home for their help on the farm. The farther the children traveled to school, the shorter the hours they could work at home. Yet it was a law that children must be confirmed, and to accomplish that end they must learn to read. Thus, the traveling system of educating children in rural Norway was set up and became firmly established throughout most of Norway by 1750.

In addition to saving the cost of building a school, there was another important advantage to the traveling school. Schooling children at home, under the watchful eyes of parents, exposed everyone to education. All those present when school was in session learned along with the children. It also served to reinforce what the older ones had learned when they were young. Once the first generation of Norwegians had learned to read, they became very supportive of compulsory education for their children when they became parents themselves.

The most common form of education provided by the local parish was the *omgangskole* (rotating or ambulatory school). According to the law, children from 7 to 12 years of age should attend school. The term was to be three months long, and the school day should last for 6 or 7 hours. Most often the school session was in the winter when the labor of children was not needed on the farm. The teacher and students met in area homes as time and space allowed, usually staying at each farm for several weeks. In a typical ambulatory school, classes were held in the largest room of the farmhouse. The teacher usually stayed with the family at whose home school was being held.

After meeting for a week or two at one farm, both teacher and pupils moved on to the next farm for another session of two or three weeks. A common complaint of the traveling teachers was that most children attended school for such a short time, that during the long interval between sessions, they forgot what they learned the previous term. Another complaint about having school in the homes was that the noise level in an ordinary household was not conducive to teaching. Often there was only one large room in the house where school was held, while all other routine household activities were ongoing. Cooking, weaving, tending babies, spinning, and other chores were carried out while lessons were being recited in that same room.

The *skoleholder*, or teacher, who traveled from one community to another was often poorly trained. In some cases, he could not even write. Usually, he (it was always a male in those days) was selected by the pastor from among the most intelligent members of the confirmation class. If he could "read good in a book," write fairly well, spell with some degree of accuracy, and be familiar with the process of arithmetic, he had all the qualifications of a top-notch teacher. If the parish had a good pastor, chances were good that he would recommend a good teacher; but in parishes where the pastor was inept, there was often a poor teacher as well.

Working conditions left much to be desired, and compensation received by the teacher left him verging on starvation. Even the most competent ones received an annual salary of only 20 *riksdaler* (silver coins equal to 4 *kroner* and used until 1875, worth about $25 today). They were paid little better than most farmhands and needed other employment to supplement the paltry sum they received for their teaching endeavors. In some parishes, the teacher was also the sexton and received a small income from that source to augment his meager teacher's salary.

Each farmer in the community was assessed a certain amount of goods to support the school and to pay the teacher. At one time it was the teacher's responsibility to collect this tithe until the system was changed in the 1800s. From that time on, the teacher was paid from taxes collected in the district by government officials.

By 1827 Norway required schools to have some of the following books: The Bible, a book of prayers, a book of hymns, the New Testament, copies of Norway's constitution and the Education Act of 1739, and an arithmetic book. The course of study was limited not only by the ability of the teacher but also by the availability (or lack thereof) of instructional materials. From *Tourist Magazine*, No. 1, 1991, we learn:

> *"When the circuit teacher traveled from farm to farm with his school satchel, there was a limit to how much he could carry with him. The children themselves had no school books, but most homes had a Bible. During school hours, the children were one by one allowed to look at one of the books the teacher brought with him. The most important teaching aid was therefore the teacher's own voice. For many generations, notebooks were too expensive to use. The children therefore formed their letters and did their sums on the cheapest possible wrapping paper."*

The lack of writing materials on which to practice, explains why most students in this parish of West Norway did not learn to write or cipher in 1820. Hafslo had a population of about 3000 people and was served by 45 traveling teachers. The teacher who was rated most highly by the minister had a total of 101 students. Of these, 20 could write, and 2 were able to cipher. Another teacher had 157 students, of whom only 5 had learned to write and none could cipher.

A school law of 1848 required every town to have a permanent common school with compulsory attendance for children beginning at the age of 7 years. The new law was heeded in the towns, and education gradually improved there, but it was considered too expensive to provide formal schooling for children of the rural districts, which included most of the children of Norway. Schooling for rural youngsters continued much as before. The only incentive for education was to learn enough to be confirmed.

A new School Act was passed in 1860, which replaced ambulatory schools with permanent schools. If there were 30 children residing within a reasonable distance to attend school on a daily basis, a school building would be erected. Prior to this time, little attention was given to subjects other than reading, writing, and arithmetic. In addition, books were to include science, history, and geography. Yet changes were slow in coming, and many rural areas still had no permanent school, so therefore the old system continued.

In the larger towns, schools were better organized and offered a broader and more advanced education than in the country. Some schools offered classical studies and served as preparatory schools for students preparing for the ministry and other professions. Laing comments on high schools in the 1830s:

> "There are five high schools in the principal towns in Norway, in which the rectors and teachers are men, such as Holmboe, Bugge, and Fresner, of known eminence as classical scholars. The student of divinity must be prepared in these schools for his professional studies and is seventeen or eighteen years of age before he is considered fit to leave them for the university."

Young men of the upper class had access to the urban high schools, however, the culmination of a rural youth's education was confirmation in the Lutheran Church. Laing comments on the importance of this rite in the training of rural youth:

> "Not being confirmed would be held equivalent to not having a character, either from want of conduct or of ordinary capacity. A young man, of the laboring class, usually took a certificate of his good character from the minister when he removed to a distant parish. The confirmation in Norway certifies much more, as in the face of the congregation, the confirmant has shown that he can read and has the use of his mental faculties to an ordinary degree, according to his station, and has moral and religious principles to direct him."

In 1864 the first folk high school was established where literature, history, and Norwegian were studied. These schools stressed the development of patriotism, personality, and character. Progress in the development of Norway's system of education continued up to the present time, making it one of the most literate countries in the world today. The education of Norway's rural population up to the late 1800s helps one to understand the lack of communication between the early immigrants in America and their relatives in Norway. Almost all of the early emigrants were educated in an omgang-skole (ambulatory school) and had not learned to write. This lack of writing skill, both in Norway and in America, made it extremely difficult for them to communicate. In light of this fact, it is more readily understood that contact between the early immigrants and their relatives both in Norway and in the United States, was meager—and often nonexistent. On occasions when letters were written, it was often a minister, teacher or other educated person who was engaged to perform this task. This perhaps explains the beautiful penmanship, as well as the formal and elaborate form of the language, used in the letters of these humble Norwegian peasants.

Chapter 8

Transportation, Travel, and Communication

Boats carrying goods and passengers have been winding their way along Norway's extensive water routes for centuries, weaving in and out among thousands of islands along the coast, and reaching far into the interior via an extensive network of long, deep fjords. For centuries this was the natural and most efficient mode of travel in West Norway and continues to be widely used today, yet boats did not satisfy all travel needs in 19th century Norway. Land travel was also necessary, though its development came slowly.

The steep mountain ranges running the entire length of the country, as well as the broad fjords and rivers penetrating far into Norway's interior, created overwhelming obstacles to the development of roads. Progress in road-building was further hampered by long winters and heavy snowfall, making it difficult not only to build but to maintain roads. The earliest routes to the interior followed the trails worn by reindeer hunters. For centuries Norwegians traveled along these narrow paths, trampled where the going was easiest, winding around marshes, ponds, bogs, boulders, and other obstacles. Herdsmen used these routes to drive cattle, sheep, and goats to mountain pastures, or to trade at inland marketplaces. Early settlements were connected in this manner, and little by little the paths were extended to become riding trails, pack roads, and where possible, cart roads; but in the most mountainous areas of the interior, footpaths and narrow trails provided the only route for travel. Some of these early primitive trails were subsequently widened and gradually improved to become the main Norwegian highways.

Walking between rocks and hard places
Anders B. Wilse/Norsk Folkemuseum

In an agrarian society, where each farm was quite self-sufficient and most of their other needs were supplied by local trade, farmers had little use for roads. The first roads were necessary only to expedite travel by government officials in carrying out their official duties. For this purpose, little more than a path, which would accommodate a pedestrian or a pack horse, was often quite sufficient.

Government officials, and those in seafaring occupations, traveled widely throughout Norway as well as to foreign countries; but most Norwegians seldom traveled far from their home communities. Yet sometimes even the peasants found it necessary to travel outside their home district to find a suitable mate for marriage, to seek better employment opportunities, to visit relatives, or to celebrate commemorative days in the lives of related family members. More extensive travel was required by the Norwegian farmer when he went to market once or twice each year to sell or barter for goods and/or services. But as a rule, travel was difficult and was not done purely for the pleasure of the traveler. However, it is a general misconception that people did not move outside their native districts in

Climbing between rocks and hard places
Anders B. Wilse/Norsk Folkemuseum

Norway. Before the time of road building Norwegians understood that *"mountains divided and the water and the valley united."* The people got around although it took far longer than we are accustomed to in the 21st century.

It was the establishment in 1647 of a postal system in Norway that gave rise to the development of a more extensive system of roads. Roads were necessary to deliver mail in the interior and to connect cities and towns of east and west Norway. By 1700 regular postal service was operating between Bergen and Trondheim, along post roads, and on most boats. Sometime after this Bergen-Trondheim route was in operation, an overland mail route was established between Bergen and Oslo (Christiania), following the Oslo-Trondheim route wherever possible. Mail was dispatched twice each week, taking about 5 days for the trip from Oslo to Trondheim. The Oslo to Bergen route required 10 days or more, barring delays due to bad weather or unfavorable road conditions.

The route from Bergen to Oslo went through Voss, to Lærdal, over Fillefjell, and down to Oslo. It was possible to go by boat from Bergen to Bolstadøyri in Evanger in 2 days. It took a day to go from Evanger to Vossevangen, and another to reach Skjerpe near Gudvangen. The post could travel by boat from there to Lærdal when conditions were favorable. However, in winter there was often dangerous ice on the fjord, so a narrow road, only a foot wide in places, was used. This greatly slowed the postman's progress. Under normal conditions, the postman arrived at Lærdal by the end of the 5th day. By the end of a week, he made it over the Fillefjell to Maristuen. Within the next few days, he arrived in Oslo. Postal rates were set according to the distance letters and parcels were sent. It was very expensive for individuals to use the postal service; however, most mail was official mail so was carried free.

Early Wooden Horse-drawn Snow Plow

As the postal service was expanded, the highway system was also expanded and improved. In 1780 the postal inspector asked the road director to improve existing roads and build a new road over the mountains between Valdres and Lærdal. Plans for the King's Road over the Fillefjell were made in 1790, and by 1800 construction was completed. The road was rough and steep, but it provided an improvement in connections between east and west Norway. This route allowed for the transport of freight over the mountains between Valdres and Lærdal.

Meanwhile, in West Norway, the general roadmaster was frustrated in his efforts at road building. In 1784 he sent a letter to his superior, complaining that it was difficult getting help to build and maintain roads. According to him, people had little desire to travel, and no interest at all in going any place they could not reach by boat. At that time the state or community required each farm, or group of farms, to build and maintain the portion of the road to which each was assigned. This was generally the portion of the road that ran through the farmer's property. Work was to be done in the spring and fall when it would not interfere with work on the farm. If the farmer did not comply, he was required to pay.

It was difficult to transport goods over steep mountain roads and trails, limiting the type of vehicle used for this work. The most efficient method of moving large and heavy objects was to do so in the winter when the frozen surfaces of rivers and lakes provided the best surface for horse-drawn sledges with heavy loads. In mountainous districts, which included much of Norway, sledges were commonly used, even in summer, as they would not tip over as easily on hillsides, nor would they roll down the mountainside. The design of wheeled vehicles was adapted to the terrain, with the wagon bed close to the ground, suspended between two wheels, and drawn by a sturdy little fjord horse.

Well into the second half of the 19th century, overland travel in the rural districts of Norway's interior was primarily by foot, walking along footpaths, cart trails, or crude roads. Pack horses or riding horses provided a common means of transport of both people and goods. Sometimes it was possible to hitch a horse to a sledge, wagon, or cart – if the road was wide enough. But in many parts of Norway carriages could not be used on rural roads until near the end of the 1800s. It was in 1848 that the first modern road was begun in Oslo. It had reasonable grades with hairpin lakeshore curves and switch-backs, making it extremely slow and expensive to build. Methods used in building roads, bridges, and tunnels, were greatly enhanced after Alfred Nobel, the Swedish chemist, developed dynamite in 1867.

Rowboat and stolkjærre

Norway depended heavily, if not entirely, on water routes for travel in many districts along the coast. Boats driven by oars, sail, and eventually steam, were widely used throughout the 19th century. Boats were also an important means of transportation on lakes and rivers of the interior, where they were also used for fishing.

Posting stations were located along the seashore or lakeshore, and served an essential function in the travel network, providing ferry service for the traveler. In addition to local boat service, there was regular service via sailing ships between Hull, England and Bergen, Norway completing the trip in three days. Steamships running between Oslo and Copenhagen were introduced in 1827. Steamship service began between Bergen and Sogn in 1844, and soon steamships connected most Norwegian seaports, and also provided service on the large lakes.

After the introduction of steam engines in Norway, railroads were developed. In 1854 the first line was opened for traffic, running from Oslo to Lake Mjøsa, a distance of 42 miles. From this modest beginning, other lines were added, so that by 1894 Oslo and Bergen were connected by rail.

Norwegian ferry boat
Anders B. Wilse/Norsk Folkemuseum

Travel Accommodations in Norway

One of the few times that a Norwegian peasant traveled any distance from home was when he had to sell goods or services, at which time he served as his own coachman. He brought his own food from home and made every effort to avoid the expense of a night's lodging, or at least keep it to a minimum. On the other hand, when government officials traveled on official trips, they were driven by others and lived comfortably. If the journey extended over several days, they took their meals at the places they stayed. Some of the facilities were clean and orderly, others were quite the opposite.

It was the law that in rural districts peasants were obliged to furnish transportation for the king, as well as for those traveling in his service. For this purpose, an ordinance was passed in 1648, establishing a system of *skyss skifter* (posting stations) across Norway. These were ordinary farms along the road or on the coastline where travelers could find boats, horses, and carts for transportation. They were to be maintained every 7 miles throughout the country. Every 21 miles there should be food, drink, and a place for the traveler to rest for the night. Horses, sledges, saddles, and other necessary equipment were to be available at each station. It is said that with a fast horse and cariole a traveler could cover 80 miles in one day.

An important position was filled by the errand boy who was to be ready, on short notice, to accompany the traveler to the next station. Although it was usually a boy (*skyss gutt*), girls were known to fill this role on rare occasions. The youngster ran alongside or sat on a platform at the back of the cart, accompanying the traveler to the next station. There the traveler got a fresh horse and cart, and the younger returned the horse and cart back to the previous station. The *skyss gutt* also acted as an errand boy, carrying *forbud* papers to the next station. These were "reservations" or orders for a horse and cart to be ready when the traveler arrived at the next station, or to alert the proprietor to have a meal or overnight accommodations prepared.

Each farmer in a given area was required to furnish a horse for use by the posting station on a given day. The horse would be delivered to the station when needed, for which the farmer received a small fee. The government made a small payment to the farmer maintaining the station, and provided additional reimbursement for the use of equipment, for services provided, and for food and drink consumed by the traveler. Income earned from the station was very meager since most travelers were government officials who traveled free. The rate charged for the use of a horse and cart or sledge from one station to another (7 miles) was about 12 skillings – approximately 10 cents. Travelers were advised to carry small coins because farmers at the posting stations seldom had change.

A farmer's obligation to provide lodging and transportation for travelers was often a great burden. During plowing, planting, harvesting, haying, or other busy times on the farm, it was an especially great inconvenience to spare people and horses for several days.

In 1851 a new law was passed which abolished obligatory posting stations. They were replaced with permanent transportation facilities which featured rooms where travelers could spend the night. The person in charge was required to keep a record of activity at his station. For this, it was necessary that he could read, write, and conduct business. If he lacked these abilities, he must have someone nearby, such as a deacon, pastor, bailiff, or sheriff who could perform these tasks for him. Government officials inspected the stations' accounts at regular intervals.

Although few people traveled in Norway purely for pleasure and amusement in the 1800s, there were some, and fortunately, they left accounts of their observations. John Ross Brown, an American who visited Norway in the 1860s, described the cariole, a two-wheeled cart, he used in his travels:

> "A little thing, with a body like the end of a canoe, perched up on two long shafts, with a pair of wheels in the rear; no springs, and only a few straps of leather for a harness; a board behind for the skydskaarl, or post-boy, to sit upon, and a horse not bigger than a large mountain goat to drag me over the road
>
> I bounced in, and stretched my legs out on each side, bracing my feet against a pair of iron catches, made expressly for that purpose."

The *karjole* was built close to the ground, so the *skyss gutt* could hop on and off the platform at the back without stopping the cart. These carts, drawn by fjord horses, small taffy-colored creatures with dark manes and tails. Fjord horses were well suited to the steep rocky roads in Norway, for they were sure-footed, strong and gentle, and required considerably less food than a full-sized horse.

Brown describes the *skyss gutt*:

> "At each station the traveler is furnished with a stunted little boy called the skydskaarl, usually clothed in the cast-off rags of his great-grandfather; his head ornamented by a flaming red night-cap, and his feet either bare or the next thing to it; his hair standing out in every direction like a mop dyed in whitewash and yellow ochre, and his face and hands freckled and sunburned, and not very clean; while his manners are anything but cultivated. The remarkable boy sits on a board behind the cariole, and drives it back to the station from which it starts."

Karjole and skyss gutt
Axel Lindahl/Norsk Folkemuseum

Skyss stations were located not only in the interior of Norway, but along the coast, fjords, and lakes as well. It was often necessary for travelers to change from land to water transport in their journey. Here one found the *jakt*, a large sloop, which was commonly used for transporting travelers, goods, and sometimes even the cart and horse. Rowboats manned by two or three rowers were used for passengers and small loads.

William Williams, from England, visited Norway in the 1850s. He traveled across much of Norway, claiming to have covered as much as 60 miles a day, crossing mountains and valleys. In an account of his experiences published in 1859, he describes conditions at stations throughout much of Norway in the early and middle 19th century. He tells:

> *"I entered a rough sort of kitchen with tables, benches, a handloom, and a great fireplace under a canopy of brick or plaster. An old woman sat curled up at the fireside — apparently hibernating. On one bench some young women and a dirty old man were eating ..."*

When Williams arrived at the station he was dressed in rough flannel clothes, hobnail boots, and had a pack on his back. The servants had taken him for a traveling tinker and gave him a room in the peasants' quarters. He was shown to a dirty double-bedded room. He described the bed as "a kind of stout coffin with some straw covered with canvas for the mattress, and a dirty rug for the covering." The wind blew in through a broken window, and Williams was unable to rest comfortably. He decided to leave and travel to the next station. His efforts to leave caused a great commotion and a relatively clean gentleman appeared. When he found out that Williams was an English traveler and not a tinker, he was shown to a clean and comfortable room. He was not offended by this mistake but rather went on at great length to praise the Norwegian peasants for the kindness they had shown him. Kindness and goodwill were evident at all times.

For breakfast, Williams was served flatbread, coffee, and cream, and then traveled on to his next destination. There he found a gloomy, dirty place. When it was time to eat he was served sour milk which he thought to be 3 or 4 weeks old, dry raw ham, and flatbread. The residents at this farm consisted of the farmer and six or seven servants. As at the previous station, the people gathered around a large wooden bowl filled with porridge and took turns dipping their spoons in it, all eating from the same bowl. The room was lighted by a torch held by the house pauper, and the old man who had to wait until the rest were finished to get his supper.

What appeared to be extremely crude and wretched travel accommodations in some parts of Norway were not exclusive to that country in the middle 1800s. Similar facilities could be found throughout much of Europe, as well as in the United States at that time.

Emily Lowe, a young lady who traveled in Norway with her mother and a French maid in the middle of the 1800s, recorded her observations in her book, *Unprotected Females in Norway*, published in 1857. She reported that conditions in some areas were unbelievably primitive, squalid, and disgusting; but in Hallingdal they were quite different. There they were greeted as welcome friends instead of strange travelers. She tells:

> *"The stations suddenly changed from the most wretched to the most comfortable Norwegian style, and cleanliness showed her fresh-washed face.*
>
> *We ran about the house in ecstasy at its cleanliness and neatness. The juniper, with which it was entirely strewed, shed a sweet odour beneath our steps, as if grateful, being there ready, at having its qualities drawn out. Solid wooden chests and curtained beds surrounded the rooms...*
>
> *All this elegance, next door to the extreme of roughness, was most unaccountable; and, though the vale was rich and fertile, we had passed through many such, without seeing any of their richness influence interiors; but the whole of this Halling district, and even the wild adjacent country into which we next branched off, combine the charms of Norwegian peculiarity and rural comfort."*

Foreign travelers complained of the people's indolence, as well as the poorly furnished sleeping quarters offered at some stations; yet they were quick to praise the Norwegians' honesty and gallantry. One traveler commented that there were no thieves and that there was little opportunity for temptation in a society where money was scarce. One traveler said that the only dishonest people in Norway were tradesmen, who sometimes cheated the peasants.

Such were travel conditions in Norway in the middle of the last century. In 1849 Thomas Bennett, a young Englishman, founded Bennett Tours, and in 1859 the first guidebook in English was published. Bennett Tours is a well-known travel bureau which is still in business.

Communication in Norway

As mentioned earlier, Norway's postal system was started in 1674, but it was not until several decades later that regular service between Bergen, Oslo, Trondheim, and Stavanger was organized. The postman traveled on foot or horseback, taking up to two weeks to carry mail from Oslo to Bergen.

Postal service in Norway was not a government affair until 1720 when it was brought directly under the Crown. Postal rates depended on the weight of the parcel and the distance traveled; but with the introduction of postage stamps in 1854, an ordinary letter could be sent any place in Norway for 4 *skilling* (about 1 cent.) From 1840 to 1886 post offices increased fourfold, and great progress was made in Norway's postal system.

January 1, 1855, the first telegraph line was opened between Oslo and Drammen. Later the same year a line had been laid to the Swedish frontier, and by 1870 lines to all of Norway were completed. The first telephone lines were completed in 1880, and by 1906 the telephone system was fairly complete throughout the country.

With her freedom from Danish rule in 1814, Norway first experienced "freedom of the press." By 1819, the first daily newspaper appeared, and vigorous development of the press followed. In 1832, when a large number of peasants were elected to the Norwegian Parliament, talented and energetic men with strong political opinions used newspapers to express their ideas and give enlightened accounts of what was happening in the world and at home. Newspapers, reviews, and periodicals were published, having a wide audience among the rural population as well as in the cities. As early as 1848, 59 newspapers and other periodicals were published in Norway.

Chapter 9

TRADING AND MARKETS

In the old rural society of Norway, farmers were known for their independence and ability to provide the most necessary services and goods on their own property. Their houses and out-buildings were made from wood and stone, materials which were found in abundance in most districts. Crops raised on the farm supplied food for both farm animals and people. Cows, goats, and sheep furnished milk and meat for the farmer's table, while the hides of horses and cattle provided leather for harnesses, shoes, clothing, and other needs. The fleece from sheep was made into woolen clothing and bedding, and flax was raised to make linen cloth.

Hedal Church door handle

Farm residents were skilled craftsmen and artisans who were capable of adapting materials at hand to their needs on the farm. Among them were gifted tailors, weavers, carpenters, blacksmiths, clockmakers, gunsmiths, locksmiths, painters, and silversmiths. The most capable woodworkers and carvers made tools, wagons, sledges, and other farm implements, furniture, chests, baskets, and various other wooden containers. Blacksmiths forged iron into horseshoes, cooking utensils, tools, parts for farm implements, and sometimes ornamental metal hinges, locks for churches, and homes.

Even though the farmer's aim was to be completely self-sufficient, this was most commonly impossible to achieve. He often needed to supplement a short supply of grain, and secure seed to plant another crop in the spring. Sometimes these needs were satisfied through barter with a neighbor, but when crops were short on one farm in the district, it was likely that other farms in the neighborhood were short also.

Skills were a marketable commodity that could be traded for the surplus goods of others, or even for money with which to purchase needed items. In lean years, special skills were far more abundant than the supply of goods. Seldom was there a bumper crop of grain creating a surplus available for sale or barter; but when there was, it was bartered for other goods or services.

In both the best and worst of times, even on the most self-sufficient farms, it was not possible to satisfy all needs and wants in the home community. Some goods and services were not available locally and, conversely, surplus products had to be disposed of through sale or trade. It was to fulfill the demand for an exchange of goods that the country marketplace was established. In order for the marketplace to function properly, there had to be roads and a means of travel, a system of comparative values, weights and measures, a medium of exchange, a scheme for marking time, a means of communication, and a system of laws.

The Market

According to law, all trade in the rural districts of Norway was to take place at the prescribed location twice each year. Farmers depended on this semi-annual market or fair to secure products such as cast iron, pottery, window glass, salt, sugar, and coffee. During years when crops failed or yields were small, people appeared at market prepared to purchase or barter for grain or flour. Products offered by local merchants and tradesmen included fish, meat, fowl, cheese, butter, flour, hides, furs, salt, cloth, grain, tar, fruit, jewelry, hardware, potash, and other merchandise.

People often came from great distances to attend market. The people of Valdres in Oppland could attend market in Christiania (Oslo), or travel over the Fillefjell to Øyri on the Sognefjord. It required several days of travel to reach either location. *Budstikken*, December 1981, published by Valdres Samband, states:

> "*These cities had their market days, when local merchants or folk were augmented by other tradesmen bringing products of the sea, the hut, the farm, the forest or shop, selling their surplus and buying their needs and wants. Perhaps they dealt through barter. The market thus grew out of a need to trade but it also became a carnival where one met old acquaintances, made new friends, bought, sold, drank, fought, and were entertained.*
>
> "*There were several market days. At 'Krossmessetid' (May 3) the first market began.*
>
> "*At the beginning the time of the market days was variable, but from 1596 on the market days began and ended at the prescribed time. They were always over before October.*
>
> "*The population of Øyri was no more than about a hundred till 1800, but the town became crowded at market when folk came from all directions. Lodging was at a premium but the folk of the area opened up their houses and sleeping men carpeted their entire floors some nights.*"

Samuel Laing, who lived near Trondheim (probably Levanger) in the 1830s, reported that a fair was held in their little town the first three weeks of December:

> "*Small vessels arrive daily with bales of dried fish, pickled herrings, and goods of all kinds, from Drontheim (Trondheim). The country proprietors from the remote glens came down with horses, cheese, butter, and other produce of their farms which they sell or barter for their year's supply of fish and groceries; but the peculiar feature of the fair is the constant coming and going of long strings or caravans of covered sledges, thirty or forty together, which in shape exactly resemble large coffins. These belong to the Jemtelanders,*

inhabiting the Swedish side of the Fjelde, about the heads of the rivers which fall into the Bothnian Gulf. They cross the Fjelde when snow has made sledge-traveling practicable, with the heaviest goods, and purchased commodities, tobacco, groceries, and all kinds of manufacturers, and the colonial produce, and fish, and transport these to the different winter fairs in the interior, as far as the Russian frontier."

Although most people brought their own food to the fair, food, ale, coffee, and sometimes stronger drink were for sale. Laing commented that the price of distilled spirits was very low, therefore he expected to observe a great deal of drunkenness at the fair, but this was usually not the case. In fact, he observed that people returning to their homes in the evening were "elevated or in liquor," but they did not cause a disturbance, and were able to take care of themselves.

Apparently, the behavior of those who attended market varied from one place to another. According to an article in *Budstikken*, market was a social event with fiddling, dancing, eating, and drinking. People from many districts gathered, often from rival communities such as Hallingdal and Valdres. It appears that fighting was considered a form of recreation in those districts at that time, so it was natural that men from the two rival valleys became combatants after having a bit too much to drink. Men from these districts had a reputation for their skill in fighting with knives and the market provided an opportunity to test their prowess in that sport.

In addition to the marketplace, goods could be purchased directly from the producer or from traveling merchants. Livestock and goods were traded or bought from the *fekar* (drover) or the *kramkar* (peddler) who traveled throughout the country. Drovers dealt in livestock. Peddlers sold household items and some imported goods. A ruling in 1746 gave drovers the right to deal in animals if they paid a certain amount of tax. The peddler's stock of goods was limited by the amount a man could carry on his back, or if he was lucky enough to have a pack horse, the amount that the horse could carry.

It was not until 1842 that stores and shops could be established in the rural areas. General trade regulations, similar to those in the towns, were introduced in the country districts through acts of 1857, 1866, and 1874. Most country markets had disappeared by 1899 when only 19 annual fairs were held in all of Norway.

Money, Weights, and Measures

Barter was the most common way of doing business at the semi-annual markets and fairs, where livestock, fish, butter, cheese, skins, hides, and cloth were used as media of exchange. In the middle of the 19th century, coins were rarely used at market by Norwegian peasants. Terms then utilized designating the value of produce and livestock, as well as volume, area, and distance, are not familiar to us today. Also, some familiar terms had a different meaning in Norway than they had in the United States.

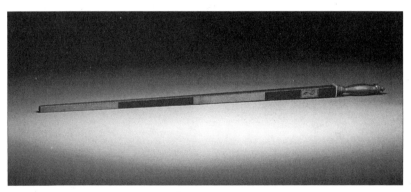

Alen measure
Vesterheim Norwegian-American Museum, Decorah, IA

Before the metric system was adopted in Norway, common linear measurements were expressed in these terms: One *alen* was equal to about 2 feet, one *fot* was equal to about 1 foot, and a *tomme* was about one inch. Until 1875, when Norway adopted the metric system, a Norwegian *mil* (mile) was equal to 7 English miles. Since then, a Norwegian mile equals 6.2 English miles or 10 kilometers. Some of the most common old words expressing weight were *bismerpund*, equal to about 12 pounds: *våg*, equal to 39.5 pounds; and *skippund*, about 350 pounds.

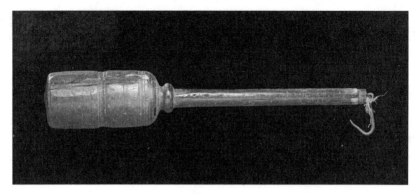

Bismer
Vesterheim Norwegian-American Museum, Decorah, IA

From the 1500s until April 17, 1875, the basic monetary unit of Norway was the *riksdaler* or *speciadaler*. The value of each varied according to the times, but after 1814 a *speciedaler* consisted of 120 *skilling*, and was equal to about one American dollar. The *riksdaler* was equal to 96 *skilling*.

Both sides of a speciadaler, 1821
Vesterheim Norwegian-American Museum, Decorah, IA

The Bank of Norway was established in 1816 and began its operation in 1818. Norway adopted the gold standard which became effective on January 1, 1874. It was the following year, 1875, when the Norwegian *krone* and *øre* were adopted and continue to be used today. There are one hundred *øre* in one *krone*. According to current values, about 8.4 *kroner* equals one American dollar (as of February 2021).

In the old Norwegian society, farms were not valued based on measured area but rather were valued in terms of how much they could produce or how much livestock they could support. One of the most unusual terms was *månedsmatbol*. This term identified the amount of land it would take to feed one man for one month. Twelve times this amount comprised a complete farm or the amount of land it took to feed one man for an entire year. A more understandable term was *mål*, which was an area measurement equal to about one-fourth of an acre.

Other terms used to express land values were based on the amount of tax levied on a certain farm. This tax was based on the farm's production and was paid in cash derived from the sale of produce. Terms used were *lauper, huder*, and *mæler*. A *laup* of butter was about 33 pounds, and one *mæl* of grain was about one-half bushel. *Hud* and *skinn* refer to tanned hides and skins. Although values varied from time to time and place to place, at one time a *laup* of butter was equal to one of the following: two cowhides, 8 goat skins, 18 sheepskins, 24 calf skins, 8 bushels barley, 10 bushels wheat, or 4 bushels of oats. A healthy 3 to 8-year-old cow with a calf was worth 4 *laup* butter (108 pounds), and a horse was worth four to six times as much.

Metric weights and measures were introduced to Norway May 22, 1875. These continue in use today.

Time Reckoning

The Julian calendar was established by Julius Caesar in 46 BC and used in Norway until 1700. The Gregorian calendar was established by Pope Gregory XIII in 1582 after he was advised by astronomers of the discrepancy between the calendar year and the solar year. Roman Catholic countries adopted the new calendar at once, but the Protestant countries continued to use the old calendar. They thought that changes made by a Roman Catholic Pope were suspect! It was not until some of the German states adopted the new calendar that Denmark and Norway began using the New Style calendar. According to this, February 19, 1700 became March 1, 1700. It was not until 1752 that England made this calendar change.

From the time that Norway was Christianized until the Reformation, ecclesiastical law required people to observe many feast days and special days to honor saints. These were commemorated by fasting, abstaining from work, and attending mass. Out of this need, a system of time reckoning evolved, the result of which was the *primstav* or calendar stick.

Calendar sticks were made of wood in a variety of shapes and sizes. Some were round, but most were made from a long narrow stick much like today's yardstick or meter stick. A small carved notch on the surface of the stick denoted each day, and larger notches marked the weeks, with special symbols indicating special feast or holy days. One side of the stick was the summer side, showing April 14 through October 13. The other side was the winter side, showing October 14 through April 13. Few people could read, but everyone was familiar with the meaning of symbols on a calendar stick.

After the formal establishment of Lutheranism in Norway in 1537, many of the formerly Catholic Saint's days or mass days lost their religious significance. Among those that survived the Protestant Reformation and continued to be important religious holidays in Norway, were the beginning of Advent, Christmas Eve, Easter, and Pentecost. Other Saint's days continued to be noted, but the less important ones gradually evolved into days marking agriculture activities on the farm.

Tradition set two annual *flyttedater* (moving days), April 14th and October 14th. On those days a servant's employment could be extended another six months if it was agreeable to both parties, or they could move to their new place of employment. Girls who were engaged in domestic service in the villages were to leave their old place at two in the afternoon and go to their new place by nine or ten in the evening. Servants wanting to emigrate were not free to leave their place of employment before April 14th. Many emigrants in the 1850s, 1860s, and later, were *husmenn* or servants, so this marked the day their term of employment was over. With their term of employment concluded, and their obligations fulfilled, they were free to leave.

Interpretation of calendar stick symbols varied from one district to another, depending on the climate and weather in the area. Some symbols and their meanings include:

CALENDAR STICK - SUMMER SIDE

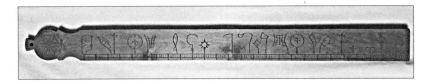

TREE – April 14 – Moving day.

ST. MARK'S DAY - April 25 - God would bless the fields

CUCKOO MASS - May 1

CROSS – May 3 – Mass of the Holy Cross. Time to begin farm work. Animals should no longer be fed inside but should be put out to graze. It was time to shear the sheep.

MILLSTONE – May 15 – St. Hallvard's Wake. Time to sow grain in some areas.

BEAR'S PAW – May 22 – St. Bernhard's Day – Bears wake up after long winter's sleep.

KOLBJØRN MED LAKSEN - June 9

BISHOP'S STAFF – June 17 – Botolv's Mass. Time for plowing and harrowing fallow fields in some districts. In Valdres the cow's milk production should be restored after short-feeding in winter.

CHURCH OR SUN – June 24 – St. John's Day – Dedicated to St. John the Baptist. Bonfires became a custom. Cows, sheep, goats, and pigs were taken to the mountain pastures.

SCYTHE – July 8 – Synneva's Day – It was time to cut hay and put on racks to dry, and fodder was collected for winter feed.

AXE – July 29. Olsok – St. Olav's Wake. Time to have haying done in the south – and time to start haying in other parts of Norway. By this time there was a lull in farm activities. Crops were growing and gates were put in place to keep the animals out of the fields. It was time for the women to thoroughly clean the house to get rid of the smoke and dirt which had collected during the winter (a good time to have a wedding!), and time for the men to check and repair roofs and hay-drying racks. In late summer, grain was cut with a sickle and bound into bunches before being put on poles to dry. When it was dry it was carried in and put in bins where it was safe from birds, mice and rats until time to thresh.

LARSOK - August 10 - Lars' Wake

MARIMESSE OM HØSTEN - August 15 - Assumption of the Blessed Virgin Mary in the Autumn.

KNIFE – August 24 – St. Bartholomew's Wake. According to old tradition, animals should be home from the mountain pastures. First day of fall – stormy weather could be expected. After everyone was home from the *seter*, the master of the farm usually had good porridge, as well as plenty to drink, for everyone at the farm. This celebration of thanksgiving marked the completion of an important part of the farm work.

NATIVITY OF THE VIRGIN MARY - September 8

CROSS – September 14 – Fall Cross Mass. Final day to leave mountain *seters*. By this time the grain must be in and gates taken down. It was time to gather twigs and leaves from trees for extra fodder. It was also time to gather nuts, herbs, and apples, as well as shear summer wool from the sheep. A second crop of hay was cut and dried before taking into the barn. This was the time to begin butchering the animals that could not be kept over the winter, and salt and cure the meat. Late in the fall, when it was cold enough so that the grain separated easily from the straw, harvesting was done.

CALENDAR STICK - WINTER SIDE

MITTEN OR POPE'S GLOVE – October 14 – Winter moving day.

SPEAR SAW AND SWORD – October 28 – St. Simon's Day. All cattle should be in, and the sleigh was brought out, for snow was expected. Time to start threshing. All animals were in their respective stalls where they remained until spring. Women should be busy making candles, spinning, weaving, knitting, mending, etc. Men made and repaired tools, utensils, and equipment; also cut wood for fuel, as well as for building.

GOOSE – November 11 – St. Martin's Day. The meat from animals butchered after this time should stay frozen.

ANCHOR – November 23 – St. Clement's Day. Time for all ships to be at anchor in the harbors.

FLAME AND BEAKER – December 13 – St. Lucia. Heavy chores to be done before Christmas must be done by this day.

SUN – December 22 – Winter Solstice. Shortest day.

DRINKING HORN OR CROWN – December 25 – Christmas Day.

3 CROSSES – January 6 – Three Kings Day. 13th day of Christmas.

AXE – January 13 – 20th day of Christmas. Church bells were rung to let everyone know Christmas was over and it was time to get back to work. The day to begin chopping wood.

SWORD OR BOW – January 20 or 25 – Paul's Mass. By this time wood for tools must be cut, for after this time, the sap began to rise in the tree.

CANDLESTICK – February 2 – Candle mass. Half of the winter's snowfall should be over. If one-half of the winter's fodder remained, there would be no shortage of fodder for the animals in the spring.

MARIAMESSE OM VÅRE - March 25

These are but a few symbols used on my calendar stick, and only a few interpretations of each are mentioned. The calendar stick was the official means of marking time until 1700 and was unofficially used until the introduction of almanacs in rural Norway in the 1800s.

Time Keeping

When my great-great-great-grandfather, Erland Knutsen Landsend, was a young man he went to Bragernes, a place south of Oslo near Drammen. In the harbor was a ship ready to sail to England. Erland took this ship and stayed in England for a while. It is reported that Erland learned a great deal on this trip, particularly about building clocks, which is demonstrated in the clocks he built when he got back to Hedalen. Before then, there was only Swedish clock-building in Hedalen, but after Erland returned from England he began to build clocks according to English design. The clocks he built in the early 1700s had weights made in exactly the same design as clock weights are made to this very day.

Erland made 28 clocks. Number 28 stood at Bronbakke in Hedalen, now at Vestre Holte in Ådalen, and had the inscription, "Erland Landsend nr. 28, 1816." Two of his clocks were *stueklokken* which he made for his two daughters. The clock he made for Sigrid was located in Etnedalen at the time of World War II. It was in a building which the Germans burned when they invaded the area. Kari Nordre Grøv's clock was the one purchased by her nephew, Halsten O. Brager, and sent to America. It is now part of the collection at the Wisconsin State Historical Museum in Madison, WI.

Clock built by Erland Knutsen Landsend in
1790 and brought to the USA by his grandson, Halsten Brager, in the 1880s.

This last-mentioned clock was a real masterpiece. It was a musical clock. The remarkable thing about it is that it plays hymns at
certain times of the day. The clockworks are made of steel and brass
which are run by 3 lead weights, one for the time, one for the striking, and one for playing the hymn tunes. It was constructed thus: A
copper roll which is run by the clockwork is fitted with steel pegs
similar to the cylinder of a music box. These pegs lift the hammers
which strike the descending plates. There are 16 hammers that make
up the musical scale. The clock first strikes the time high on a bell,
soon thereafter it plays a hymn tune. The clock plays four tunes alter-
nately every sixth hour in this manner. At one o'clock at night it plays

"Jeg vil din pris utsjunge i denne morgenstund"—at 7 a.m. *"Hvad kan oss komme til for nød"*—at 1 p.m. *"Når tid og stund der er for hånd"*—and at 7:00 in the evening *"Den lyse dag forgangen er."*

The dial is artistically made. It is of brass with a circle of pewter upon which are engraved the hours and minutes which are black.

A grandson of Erland Fossholtsmeden, Halsten O. Brager was also a watchmaker and had a large watch-making business in America. He was home in Hedalen in 1884 where he purchased the clock his grandfather, Erland Knutsen Landsend, had made for his daughter Kari Nordre Grøv. Halsten had the clock shipped to the United States in 1884. The clock was in the H. O. Brager family until it was taken to the University's antique collection in Madison, Wisconsin, where it is at the present time.

Chapter 10

EMIGRATION FROM NORWAY

Norwegian Emigration 1825-1930

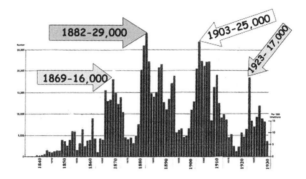

The first white explorer to reach North America is believed by many to be the Viking explorer, Leif Eiriksson, in the year 1001. Other Norsemen are said to have settled briefly on American soil in the 11th century. Norwegians were among the colonists who first settled along the eastern coast of the United States in the 1600s, but it was not until 1825 that Norwegian emigration began. Before that time the only Norwegians in America came to this country as individuals or single families and were absorbed into the existing settlements along the east coast.

Since the time of Colonial America, most immigrants in the United States came from England, the Netherlands, France, Germany, and Ireland; but in the 19th century, large numbers of immigrants from northern and western Europe began arriving in America. People were driven from their homelands by famine, revolution, and political unrest. The most familiar catastrophe of the time was the potato famine in Ireland, during which a large percentage of her population went to America. Norway was second only to Ireland in the percentage of its total population to leave the homeland and emigrate to the United States.

Cause of Emigration from Norway

New farm implements and methods appeared in Norway in the middle and late 1700s, and new crops were introduced, most importantly – the potato. These agricultural improvements provided better nutrition. This, plus the enactment of the smallpox vaccination law in 1810, resulted in more infants and children surviving to adulthood. The population in Norway increased due to improvements in the general health of the people who then lived considerably longer.

The small amount of tillable land in Norway was inadequate to produce enough food for the increased population. Crop failure often decimated an already insufficient harvest, forcing some people to grind a layer of bark from certain trees to add to their meager supply of flour. Others ate moss and grass to survive. Rich and poor alike suffered. Severe economic depression and the imposition of heavy taxes left many farmers unable to raise money to buy out their siblings, pay the required pension to their retired parents, or pay their debts. Wealthy landowners were burdened with taxes to such an extent that it was necessary to sell a part, or sometimes all, of their land to pay the heavy taxes. People of the rural classes were oppressed by the upper class, and tithes and taxes, required by church and other government officials, could not be paid. Many farms fell into the hands of money-lenders or the sheriff.

Few opportunities for profitable employment existed for young people. Their wages were deplorable. For instance, a farmhand received an annual salary of only $10 or $20. Poor economic prospects in rural Norway made life intolerable for many people. It was in this predicament, between a rock and a hard place, that a great many people found themselves in the middle of the 1800s. It is told that some people left Norway for religious reasons or to escape military service, however, they were the exception, not the rule. It was the rapid growth of the population during a period of economic hardship that drove most Norwegians from their homeland. They left Norway in search of a better life and improved living conditions.

Up until that time, most people had few choices other than accepting things as they were. During the first half of the 1800s Norwegians heard about vast tracts of fertile soil and cheap land available in the United States. Soon emigrants began leaving Norway and going to the United States. They sent messages back to relatives and friends in Norway telling of the opportunities they found in America. Word reached even the most remote valleys of Norway, resulting in a frenzy to emigrate which became known as "America Fever."

The First Emigrants

The first organized group of emigrants to leave Norway sailed out from Stavanger on July 4, 1825, on the sloop, *Restauration*. Onboard were 45 passengers and a crew of 7. In his book, *The Promise of America*, published in 1984, Odd Lovoll describes the vessel as being about 39 tons, 54 feet long, and 16 feet wide. (For comparison purposes, the *Mayflower*, the ship that brought the Pilgrims to America in 1620, weighed 180 tons, was 90 feet long, and had about 100 people on board.)

The *Restauration* - the first emigrant ship
Vesterheim Norwegian-American Museum, Decorah, IA

The *Restauration* arrived in New York on Sunday, October 9, 1825, after 98 days at sea. Not only did everyone on board survive the trip across the ocean, but there was also an increase in the number of passengers. A baby girl was born during the journey. This group of immigrants, who are often referred to as "The Sloopers," founded the Kendall settlement in the state of New York with limited success, and during 1834 and 1835 most of the settlers left New York and moved to northern Illinois. There they purchased land and founded the Fox River settlement in LaSalle County, IL.

In 1836, eleven years after the first organized group emigrated, the next large emigrant group left Norway. Two brigs left Stavanger in the spring, one with 110 passengers, the other with 57. The following year, two more ships sailed for America with a total of 175 emigrants. Most of the people who emigrated in 1836 and 1837 settled in the Fox River region of Illinois. From that time forward, emigration from Norway to America became an annual occurrence.

The *Hebe*, built in Norway
Fast and used more than any other ship between 1856-1868.
Vesterheim Norwegian-American Museum, Decorah, IA

One of the early immigrants in Illinois, Ole Rynning, wrote a book that contained advice to prospective emigrants and provided detailed descriptions of conditions in America. *A True Account of America*, published in Norway in 1838, was widely distributed throughout the rural districts of Norway and became the most influential guidebook during the early years of emigration. In addition to Rynning's book, information was circulated through letters, newspaper articles, and also first-hand accounts reported by returned travelers who had been to America.

Many officials and most clergymen in Norway opposed emigration. Officials gave lengthy speeches and published articles that pointed out the dangers of emigrating, while pastors delivered sermons filled with threats and warnings of what lay ahead for the unwary emigrants. The disadvantages and pitfalls of emigration, as described by opponents of the movement, were equally as inaccurate as were the grossly overstated advantages advocated by proponents of emigration. Regardless of how blustery the controversy became in Norway, the miserable condition of Norway's peasantry did not improve, and many people felt they had nothing to lose by leaving Norway and going to America.

Norway's shipbuilders had been building seaworthy vessels for centuries. Her navigators had been successfully plying the seas since Viking times, and her seamen traveled to the far corners of the world; however, most of Norway's rural people knew little of the world outside their home community. They lived in relative isolation, not only from the rest of the world but also from other districts in Norway. Yet, their lack of first-hand knowledge of the world outside did little to deter them. They were not only eager, many were desperate to improve their condition. Might it have been from their Viking forefathers that they inherited an aggressive quality in their character and an innate spirit of adventure? It is something to ponder, for had they been a timid lot they might never have left Norway.

Almost all of the early Norwegian emigrants were of the rural class. The first to leave had enough money to purchase their passage and perhaps a few acres of land, but many of those who emigrated later received money for passage to America from a relative already established in a Norwegian immigrant community in the United States. None of the early Norwegian emigrants would be considered wealthy. Even the land-owning farmers were of modest means.

If we are to believe what O. N. Nelson writes, all those who emigrated from Norway were capable and honest people. In his book, *History of the Scandinavians in the United States*, published in 1893, he stated:

> "*Criminals, paupers, and idiots are cared for by the Northern governments and are not permitted to leave. The poor and vicious classes cannot pay for their own passage nor receive a ticket on credit. Cowards dare not and fools have not enough sense to emigrate.*"

It is interesting to contemplate the emotions involved in deciding to leave Norway in the middle 1800s. Despite a compelling urge to emigrate and confidence in the safety of the journey, the actual departure was a traumatic experience for most emigrants. It was only after carefully and deliberately considering all options that Norwegians decided to leave home and family, never to see either again. With dignity and determination families disposed of all livestock and possessions they would not need in their new home. A traveler in Norway in the 1860s reported that many heirlooms were sold to secure passage money for America. What remained of their worldly goods was carefully packed in sturdy trunks and containers to accompany them on their journey to America.

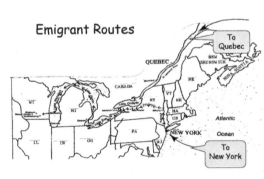

Emigrant Routes

Illustration of Immigrant Routes in North America.

The first Norwegian emigrants to America entered the country through ports in the eastern United States, usually New York. Emigrant ships carrying Norwegians continued to arrive in New York and other harbors of eastern United States until about 1850 when their main port of entry shifted to Quebec in Canada.

Britain repealed her Navigation Acts in 1849 so that ships of all nations were permitted to land in Canadian ports. Norwegian ships first began arriving in Quebec in 1850, and by 1853, 90% of all Norwegian immigrants entered America through that port. Fares from Norway to New York were up to $40 per person, but from Norway to Quebec they were considerably cheaper. An adult could travel to that Canadian port for $12 to $30. Those under 12 or 14 years of age paid half that amount, and babies under 1 year traveled free with their parents.

Ticket prices from Norway to America

1846 --------------------------- 20 spd.*

1853 --------------- Stavanger to Quebec
Adult .... 14 spd
Under 18 .... 10 spd.
Under 12 .... 8 spd.
1-6 years .... 6 spd

1866 --------------- Norway to Chicago
Steam .... 48-50 spd.
Under 12 .... ½ fare

*1 spd (spesiedaler) worth about 1 USD

Example of a passenger ticket from Bergen
to Quebec in 1866.

Norwegian ships brought immigrants to Canada and carried timber back to England. From there, miscellaneous cargo was carried to other ports, eventually returning to Norway where preparations were made for a spring departure with another load of emigrants bound for America.

Preparation for the Journey to America

Preparation for the journey began well ahead of the time for emigration. Each family was required to provide their bedding and food for the journey, which was expected to last 6 to 16 weeks, depending on route and weather. Animals were butchered and the meat was dried or salted, flour was ground, flatbread baked, cheese made, and butter churned. Imagine the volume of food required for a family with six children. At home in Norway, they were accustomed to eating three or four times a day, but it is doubtful they ate that often aboard ship. It was necessary to make containers to store and transport all of the food for the journey, and to build sturdy wooden chests with iron

Seljestad Station
Axel Lindahl/Norsk Folkemuseum

bands to safely carry the most treasured possessions to their new home in America. Everything not essential to the trip was sold or given away, and at last, the emigrant was ready to leave.

April was the usual time to sign out of the congregation in Norway, but some signed out earlier. By leaving in early spring migrants might arrive at their destination in the United States early enough in the summer to plant a crop and prepare a dwelling house before the cold weather set in. Mid-April was the most convenient time for farm servants to emigrate. As stated previously, these servants were hired for six months at a time, the winter term from October 14 to April 13, the summer term from April 14 to October 13. Service was ended or renewed on those dates.

If there was still snow on the ground when the emigrants were ready to begin their journey, sleds were used to transport their provisions to the nearest waterway. If there was no snow, carts and pack horses were used. The easiest way to travel was by boat, so that method of transportation was used whenever possible.

It was often the case that a large number of people emigrated from the same district at the same time. Agents visited the emigrants in their home community to assist in securing tickets and making other necessary travel plans. It was very important to plan the schedule carefully to make certain a ship was available for boarding as soon as they reached the port from which they would leave Norway, and that their valuable stock of food was not reduced while waiting to board a ship.

Early sailing ships carried from 80 to 150 emigrants as well as cargo. Baggage was placed on top of the cargo, and passengers had crude bunks between decks. Cooking was done on deck in good weather, but during bad weather, little cooking was done and food preparations were meager.

Norway had excellent sailing vessels and her sailors were well trained, so most people made it to America safely. Shipwrecks were rare, and most deaths that occurred on board ship were due to illness and disease. The most common ailment suffered by the emigrants was seasickness, from which recovery was generally quite fast; however, crowded and unsanitary conditions contributed to the spread of disease and other illnesses. It is said that about 3% or 4% of Norwegian emigrants died before reaching their destination in America. Exactly how many of them died as a direct result of emigration is not known. Perhaps some would have died even had they not emigrated.

Those who thought their journey was ended when they reached America were badly mistaken. Several more weeks of difficult travel lay ahead. Various means of travel were employed by the immigrants in the United States, including boats, railroads, oxen or horses, and walking. Fear of shipwreck did not end when an immigrant reached America. Storms on the Great Lakes were frequent and often severe in spring and summer. Additional problems were presented at each stopping-place along the route to the interior, where tricks and frauds lay in wait for the unsuspecting immigrants. Unscrupulous people were often successful in cheating the immigrants out of what remained of their limited financial resources. Sometimes these were their own countrymen, but more often it was an American who took advantage of the immigrants' inability to understand the English language. Some Norwegians arrived at their destination with a small amount of money, some with no money, and others were in debt.

Ninety percent of all Norwegians that came to America arrived after the Civil War ended in 1865, however, most of my husband's and my emigrant ancestors left Norway before the Civil War began. The first of our ancestors immigrated in 1843, and the last one in 1880. Those who emigrated before 1860 left Norway as family units as was customary at that time. Those who left Norway as unmarried young adults traveled in the company of one or more of their siblings.

Our earliest ancestors first settled in Koshkonong, Dane County, Wisconsin, one of the most important of the early Norwegian immigrant communities in this country. As that settlement became saturated with immigrants, they sold their farms and moved north and west to the newer Norwegian immigrant settlements in the townships of Perry and Vermont, which were also in Dane County, Wisconsin. Those who emigrated from Sogn and Valdres in the 1850s and 1860s settled in Vermont Township, with one exception. One family from Valdres lived in Adams Township, Green County, Wisconsin, until the 1880s when they moved to Vermont Township. Those who came from Voss in the late 1860s and 1870s went to Worth County, Iowa. Our last immigrant ancestor came from Sogn in 1880. He came to Freeborn County, Minnesota, where he lived for a short time before settling in Worth County, Iowa.

Perhaps the greatest difference in the experiences of the first of our ancestors to leave Norway and the last was in the emigrant journey. The majority of our ancestors came by sailing ship to America. Those who came before 1854 landed in New York, and those who came between 1854 and the end of the 1860s landed in Quebec, Canada. Only the last ones to immigrate experienced the luxury of traveling by steamship.

Family Emigrant Journeys to Wisconsin

My own ancestors were Norwegian emigrants who came to America between 1852-1869. They brought trunks, containers, documents, memorabilia, circumstances, and accounts of their journeys some of which are described here.

1857 Johannes and Martha Urness Journey

An emigrant trunk with rosemåling, brought to the
United States in 1857.

Among those who left Norway were my paternal great grandparents who came from the Urness farm in Sogn. Johannes Hansen Urness emigrated with Martha and their 1½-year-old daughter, Anna, in 1857. Their belongings were packed into two big rosemaled trunks, including the one pictured on the previous page, and a little red trunk. They signed out of the parish on 11 April 1857. The date on Johannes' trunk is 1855, the year he planned to emigrate. However, when they discovered that Martha was pregnant, the trip was delayed until 1857. This is explained in the following attest translated here:

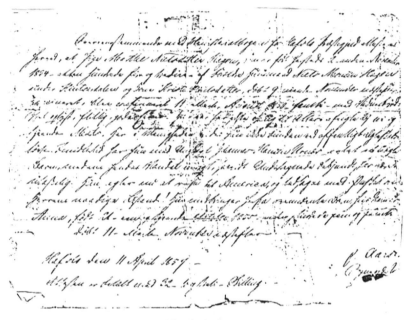

Martha's Attest

"This is to certify that according to the church record at Hafslo Prestegjheld Martha Nilsdatter Hage was born here 2 November 1834. Parents - fatherhusband Nils Monsen Hagen under Kintzerdalen, mother Kristi Polsdatter. Martha was baptized 9 Nov 1834. Vaccinated 1838. Confirmed 11 August 1850 with witness. She was well raised and intelligent, ambitious and clever. She took communion the last time this year 29 March 1857. Here in the parish she is not known to be bound to any engagement. In the meantime she has had a baby out of wedlock with the young man Johannes Hansen

Urnes, and has not had any other affairs. She now plans to go to America with the Lord's blessings. She is taking with her the aforementioned baby whose name is Anna, born 21 October 1855, and baptized 11 November 1855. Signed, P. Aars, Sogneprest. Hafslo the 11 April 1857. This certificate is paid for with 32 skilling. (About 25 cents)"

They left their home on the shore of the Luster fjord in Sogn in a small boat that took them to Solvorn on the west shore of the fjord. There they boarded a bigger boat that traveled through the fjord and down the coast of Norway to the port city of Bergen. At the police station in Bergen, Johannes' passport was issued on Friday, 17 April 1857, and Martha's and the baby's issued the next day. Martha's passport reads:

Police Chief in the Cathedral City of Bergen Norway.

Martha Nielsdatter Hagen with her 1½ year old baby girl plans to go from this city where there is no contagious disease to America. It is my duty to let her on this trip without interference. Age 23 years old, medium height, dark hair, blue eyes, no birthmarks.

18 April 1857

They boarded an emigrant sailing ship in the harbor, and left Bergen on Monday, 20 April 1857, and sailed to Quebec, Canada. At Quebec they transferred to a boat that passed through the St. Lawrence Seaway and the Great Lakes to Milwaukee, where they took the train to Black Earth, Wisconsin. It was mid-summer when they arrived at their final destination – the home of Martha's uncle, Lars Munson. Lars had been in America for 10 years and owned a farm three miles south of Black Earth.

An example of how one little primitive artifact stimulated my curiosity to learn about its origin was this flour box here. Johannes told his grandson (my father, Nels) that he brought it from Norway in 1857 and during the ocean voyage, the flour in this box had weevils, which were not uncommon. The flour could still be used in baking because the high temperatures killed the weevils making the food safe to consume.

Flour box brought to Wisconsin
from Sogn in 1857.

1857 Anderson/Skinningsrud Journey

An early family emigration is that of my great-great-grandparents, Anders and Gjertrud who went by either the patronym Anderson or Skinningsrud, the farm name. They came from Valdres to Wisconsin in 1857. With the help of an emigration agent arrangements were made well in advance of the journey. They sold their farm in Hedalen to Andrew's brother, Iver, in 1856 for about 400 dollars. The price of tickets from Norway to Quebec on a sailing ship varied. However, according to oral tradition, Anders and Gjertrud used about one-half of the proceeds from the farm for travel expenses, and the other half was saved to purchase land when they arrived at their destination.

Anders Anderson

Gjertrud Anderson

Olaug Christensdatter Skinningsrud

The Hedal church records in Valdres show that the extended family signed out of the congregation to go to America. Heading the family was the matriarch, Olaug, who was 65 years old and had been a widow for 25 years. She was born in 1792 in Hedal, Norway, and died in Wisconsin in 1880 at the age of 88. Some of her sons emigrated in 1853 and were already established as farmers in Wisconsin. In addition to Olaug, the family group emigrating in 1857 consisted of her daughter Gjertrud and husband Andres and their 6 children, ages 10-18; her son Østen and wife Ingeborg and their three children, ages 2-10; and 2 unmarried daughters, Olaug and Berit, ages 33 and 35.

At that time emigrants were required to furnish their own food, bedding, cooking utensils, and other provisions to last for the duration of the journey. The emigrants loaded their belongings on hand carts (or sleds if there was still snow on the ground) for the approximate 85 mile trip from their farm in the Valdres Valley to the seaport at Drammen, in the Oslofjord. Roads in Norway were little more than cart tracks in 1857, but lakes, rivers, and fjords offered boats for hire whenever possible. It is most likely that a boat at the Begna River carried them to the southern tip of Spirellen, where they traveled overland to Tyrifjorden. After crossing the fjord they continued the last few miles overland to Drammen, the seaport where they boarded the waiting sailing bark, *Balder*, under Captain Haagensen. From shipping records on the internet, I learned that the *Balder* left Drammen on May 2nd and arrived in Quebec on June 26, 1857.

Information about their journey from Quebec to Wisconsin was discovered in a recent volume of Norwegian immigrant letters that were found, translated, and published in 2012 by the Norwegian American Historical Association in Northfield, MN: *From America to Norway – Norwegian-American Immigrant Letters Volume One, 1838-1870*. On page 228 in this book of letters compiled by Orm Øverland, Torgrim Olsen Lee writes to his family in Norway from Black Earth, Dane County, Wisconsin on 24 July 1857. The letter was addressed to Anders Olsen Lie, Hedalen, Sør Aurdal, Oppland, and describes the emigrant journey on the *Balder* with my Anderson ancestors from Hedalen in Valdres. In this letter he tells the following:

"To our dear parents and siblings in Norway:

Now that we've arrived (in Wisconsin) I have the opportunity and I'll write you some simple lines and tell you about our journey to America. We were at sea for seven weeks and six days and we stayed on board the ship for four days after anchoring in Quebec before we arranged for our further journey. We had one price from Quebec to Madison but had to change conveyance four times; thirteen and a half dollars for every adult and half price for those under twelve. We went by railroad, a very fast transportation. It was more than 700 miles and it took us four days and nights. In Madison, we bought our tickets to Black Earth. It was a happy moment because there we were met by old friends, all of the Skindingsrud boys. Knut, Peter, and Ole Brager,

Gulbrand Berg, Halsten Norby, Arne, Ole, Andreas, and Anders Steensrud, and many more each took care of his own."

The four Skindingsrud boys referred to in this letter were Olaug's four sons, Christian, Ole, Paul, and Peter Paulson (or Skinningsrud) who had emigrated several years earlier. They met the new arrivals at the train depot in Black Earth and took them to their homes, where they lived until finding land and establishing homes for themselves.

The emigrants went by river steamer from Quebec to Hamilton, by rail on the Great Western RR from Hamilton to Detroit, the Michigan Central RR from Detroit to Chicago, and the Chicago, Milwaukee, St. Paul, and Pacific Railroad to Madison. The line to Prairie du Chien passed through Black Earth in time to accommodate the Anderson/Skinningsrud party in 1857.

Anders and Gjertrud Anderson and their family settled on 160 acres in Green County, Wisconsin. Their son, Andrew was living there when he met Kari Olsdatter Brager who was 21 years old when she emigrated from the same parish in Norway with 2 of her brothers, in 1861. Young Andres and Kari were married in 1862. In 1884 Andrew and Kari and their children, as well as Andrew's parents, moved to Vermont Township in Dane County where they spent the rest of their lives.

1864 Young Ole Brager Journey

Ole Olson Brager, 28, a brother of Kari (young Andrews's wife above), emigrated in 1864 with his 26-year-old wife and their 2 little daughters, one 3 years old and the other 7 months. They also came from Hedalen to the immigrant community in Wisconsin. Some of the hardships of their emigration are described in a letter written by Ole after he arrived in Black Earth, Wisconsin, in 1864:

"The first of May we sailed out from Christiania (Oslo) and came to Quebec 21 June. We had it very nice on the boat, but twice there were storms, once on the North Sea and again on the Banks of Newfoundland. The wind was so strong at night that there was not a whole sail left in the morning. Heavy ropes and iron chains broke and we found many big

fish washed on the deck by the big waves. We saw lots of whale and other sea creatures. Many of the people were sick most of the trip but Marit (his wife) and I were healthy the whole time. Kari was sick for 5 days when she wasn't able to be up. But the rest of the trip we were all right.

We arrived at Quebec without enough money to go farther. I borrowed $10 and still we needed $10 more to get to Chicago, so the captain loaned it to me. When we were ready to go, the captain asked if we had any money left to use on the trip, and we told him we did not. He said it would not be good to travel without the means to buy anything for the children, so he got permission from his wife to give $10 to those who did not have anything."

Young Ole Olsen Brager joined the Union Army in November, four months after arriving in America. He became ill and was hospitalized in Madison, Wisconsin, and there he died of disease on May 11, 1865, less than one year after arriving in America. He left a 27-year-old widow and two daughters.

1869 Ole E. & Kari Grøv Brager Journey

Steam travel to America began in the 1860s, and fares were greatly increased so a much shorter time was required for the journey. All 8 of my great grandparents came from Norway on sailing ships between 1852-1861, before the Civil War. In 1869, after the war, my great-great-grandparents, Ole E., age 63, his wife, Kari, age 55, and their youngest son, Christopher, age 16, came to America on the maiden voyage of the *Idaho,* one of the earliest trans-Atlantic steam plus sail ships that carried emigrants. They left Christiania (Oslo) on a British feeder ship Friday evening, the 9th of April, and arrived in Hull, England Monday, the 12th of April. They immediately crossed England by rail to Liverpool where they boarded the steam/sail ship, *Idaho.* The next day, Tuesday, April 13, they left Liverpool and arrived in New York April 30 – after 17 days at sea. The total amount for tickets from Oslo to Madison, WI cost $44.50 each and included "Norwegian service and free food." The only cash they had was 10 *specidaler*. As they were said to be very poor, apparently their 8 children living in the USA contributed to the cost of prepaid tickets for them to emigrate. This route, from Norway to Hull, across England to Liverpool, and from there to the USA was the usual route followed by Norwegians until Norway had her own steamship company.

The last sailing ship to carry immigrants to America left Norway in 1873. From that time on, emigrant ships were powered by steam engines, and from New York, one could travel by railroad to the Norwegian immigrant communities of the Midwest.

The emigrant journey is often thought of as being extremely difficult, and a grim experience. For some emi-

Ole E. & Kari Grøv Brager

grants, this was, indeed, the case. Many others experienced pleasure on the ship, as well as on the trip to the interior. When the weather was good there was dancing on the deck of the ship. Games were played, church services were held, and much time was spent comparing information and ideas of what the future held. Life-long friendships and romances were established during the long hours at sea, as well as on the overland journey.

Another misconception is that the Norwegian emigrant traveled alone to America. This is unlikely. Early emigration from Norway was mostly a family emigration, including the father, mother, and children; and sometimes grandparents, aunts, uncles, cousins, and other relatives. Often other acquainted families and individuals from the home parish in Norway traveled in the same emigrant group, and to the same destination in the United States where they would join earlier immigrants, often relatives from the old country.

Chapter 11

THE NORWEGIAN IMMIGRANT COMMUNITY IN THE UNITED STATES

The first Norwegian immigrant community in the United States was founded in Kendall County, New York in 1825. Some of the settlers moved to LaSalle County, Illinois, in 1834, and by 1836 Norwegians had settled in Chicago. In 1837, Norwegian settlements appeared at Beaver Creek in Illinois, and the following year Norwegians were living in Shelby County, Missouri.

The first Norwegians to come to Rock County, Wisconsin arrived in 1838. In 1839, they formed the Muskego settlement in Waukesha and Racine Counties and in 1840 the Koshkonong (known as Kaskeland in Norwegian) settlement in Dane County was established. Koshkonong became the most important settlement of Norwegians in Wisconsin.

According to Martin Ulvestad, in *Nordmendene i Amerika*, 18,200 people emigrated from Norway between 1825 and late 1850. In 1850, 10,000 Norwegians were living in Wisconsin. Of those, about 3,300 of them resided in Dane County and, of those, 75% lived in the Koshkonong settlement. As that settlement became saturated, the overflow moved north and west to form large settlements in Wisconsin, Iowa, Minnesota, and eventually into the Dakota Territory. The first Norwegians in Iowa were those who settled at Washington Prairie in Winneshiek County in 1850. Fillmore County, Minnesota became the first Norwegian settlement in that state in 1852. Seven years later, in 1859, Norwegians arrived in Dakota Territory and established a settlement near what is now Vermillion, South Dakota. It was 1880 before they established settlements in North Dakota. Groups of Norwegians lived in Michigan, Nebraska, and elsewhere;

but during the early decades of immigration, the main settlements were those in Illinois, Wisconsin, Iowa, and Minnesota.

The spread of Norwegian settlements to the west was greatly enhanced by the development of railroads. In 1854, the railroad from Chicago reached Rock Island on the Mississippi River, and another line was completed to Madison, Wisconsin. This line reached Prairie du Chien by 1857 and, in 1858, there was a railroad to LaCrosse, Wisconsin. The first railroad appeared in Minnesota in 1862 and by 1870 one could travel to the Red River Valley by rail.

A Typical Immigrant Community

This chapter portrays life in a typical rural Norwegian-American settlement during the early decades of immigration. It deals mainly with the Norwegian immigrant community in Vermont Township, Dane County, Wisconsin, during the 1850s and 1860s. It is typical of other settlements at that time when most Norwegian immigrants came from farms in Norway and settled on farms in Illinois, Wisconsin, Iowa, and Minnesota.

It is extremely difficult to imagine what the early Norwegian immigrants experienced while making new homes for themselves in America. Few accounts tell the story in the immigrants' own words, because most rural Norwegians could not write at that time. They were taught to read the Black-letter or Old English script found in Norwegian books, but only ministers, teachers, some officials, and a few other educated people, could write or read handwriting. The immigrant had to rely on one of those people to write letters home, as well as read letters received from Norway. Firsthand accounts of life in the Norwegian immigrant community were often written several, if not, many years after the fact. Some events were recorded during a moment of melancholy, with ordinary incidents elaborately embroidered with magnified details. Other accounts were written by a proud penman with more concern for a lofty literary style than with accuracy, or by a writer who thought the mundane details of everyday life were not worthy of mention. However, by consulting a multitude of resources, one can get a fairly accurate picture of the early Norwegian immigrants' lives.

Cradle brought from Hadeland to the immigrant
community in Dane County, Wisconsin, in 1852.

As newcomers on the American frontier, Norwegians soon discovered that not all rocks and hard places had been left behind in
Norway. They found hardships and suffering in America too, much of
which was a fact of life at that time, be it in Norway or in in America.
Many immigrants had a difficult time adjusting to a strange country
with an unfamiliar language and customs, extremes of temperature
and weather, and alien farming methods and crops. With diligence
and industry, they persevered in their effort to stay healthy of mind
and body while building a new life for themselves. In most cases,
they were rewarded. Their endeavors in the United States resulted in
a marked improvement in their circumstances; an opportunity they
would not have had in the Old Country.

The Immigrants' First Home

When Norwegians set out for the United States, they knew where
they were going. In most cases, they were going to one of the Norwegian immigrant settlements where a relative, friend, or neighbor, was

already established. They arrived with only a few tools, and the most basic necessities of life packed away in their round-topped emigrant chests. Until they could build their own house, they were given shelter with a relative or friend from the home community in Norway.

Anna Urness' little red trunk brought from Norway in 1857

Johannes and Martha Urness, mentioned in Chapter 10, were not married until they had been in Wisconsin for several months. They were married, on Monday, 21 December 1857, by the Norwegian immigrant pastor who had been called to serve the immigrant communities in the Blue Mounds area. Pastor Peter Marius Brodahl arrived from Norway in July 1856 to serve the congregations in Vermont, Springdale, Perry, and North Blue Mounds townships. Along with baptizing 142 infants, Johannes and Martha were one of the twenty-one couples he married during the following year. Their daughter, Anna, was then 2 years old, and Martha was expecting their second child. They had been in Wisconsin for five years when Johannes bought part of the farm from Martha's uncle in 1862. In September 1864, Johannes was drafted into the Union Army, leaving his wife, Martha, and four children: Anna 9, Brita 6, Christina 3, and Hans 1, living at the Monsen farm in Wisconsin, while he went off to fight in the Civil War. Nine months later, the war ended and Johannes was mustered out of the army. He returned to Wisconsin in June 1865, having earned enough money as a soldier to purchase more of the farm. Their son, Hans, was my grandfather, and his son,

Nils, was my father. I was born and grew up on that same farm in Wisconsin, which is now owned by my nephew Jon Urness.

Johannes and Martha's log home in Wisconsin in 1880 and enlarged in 1883
Illustration by Mattie Urness and artistic interpretation by Sue Webber

One of the first things they did was locate land that was for sale and record their intentions to purchase it at the land office. Many of the early immigrants were prepared to pay cash for land when they arrived in this country, but others had to work as hired men or day laborers until they could save enough money for land. The going rate for a day's work was 50 cents, an amount that was unheard of in Norway. What would have been a farm servant's annual salary in Norway could be earned in America in one month.

In *Samband*, a magazine written in the Norwegian language and published by Valdres Samband, A. L. Lien wrote a series of articles in 1913 dealing with the Blue Mounds Settlement in northwestern

Dane County, of which Vermont Township was a part. The following is a translation from that source:

> "All who came, and had some money left after the immigrant journey, first purchased land, and all who had a family must have a cow and oxen. It was seldom that those who came with families were completely without money, and many had what at the time was considered a lot of money. When they had paid for their land, secured a house, oxen and cows, plow, stove, and other equipment, the purse became very small. All began with farming and the first task was to produce something for provisions. The summer they arrived was devoted to raising a crop, but in winter they must make rails and build fences, and cut logs for a house if they had not put up a house in the fall. When May came, they plowed up some land and planted it with grain, usually resulting in a good harvest. This provided grain for flour and feed for the pigs in the fall. Dairy products provided much of the food for the Norwegians as they were better skilled in producing and utilizing milk than anything else. Everyone lived in the same manner – those who had less wealth were equal to those who had more when everyone did his share.
>
> Everyone worked early and late, six days a week, and rested Sunday, doing only what was necessary on that day. If anyone was sick, the neighbors helped out. Doctors were seldom called because they were so far away. If the neighborhood had received crops enough for bread and seed they were not forced to sell their crops in the fall and buy bread and seed in the spring. If they were short of grain in the fall, and could not get a threshing machine right away, the men went to a neighbor and borrowed a few bushels of wheat and paid with the same when they got their crop threshed."

Many immigrants secured government land by the right of pre-emption, which was established by an act of the United States Congress in 1841. A settler filed a land application and moved to the property. If he stayed there for six months and improved it, he could then purchase it for $1.25 an acre. Later the Homestead Act of 1862 made land available free to citizens, and aliens intending to become citizens, who were over 21 years of age and the head of a family. If they lived on the land for 5 years and improved it, they would obtain title for 160 acres. Established farmers also took advantage of this opportunity. They sold their improved farms in Wisconsin at a considerable profit and moved west to where homestead land was available. The profits from their first farm could then be invested in livestock and machinery.

The most important task the first year was to break a few acres of land and plant a crop to assure their survival the first winter in America. Those who arrived too late to plant a crop had to use their small reserve of funds to borrow from others to see them through to the next spring.

Equally as important as planting a crop was providing shelter. The most efficient way to do this was to dig a hole in a hillside, close up the front of the hole with timbers, and cover it with a roof of birch bark and sod. A door and a window or two were built into the front wall. The floor of the dugout was packed dirt. A fireplace of stone was built into one of the corners to provide heat as well as fire for cooking.

Although dugouts were frequently built, the immigrant's first home was more often of log construction. It was a small structure, similar in size and design to those occupied by cotters in Norway, seldom more than 12' x 14'. Those little huts often housed not only the owner and his family but sheltered relatives and friends who were new arrivals from Norway. Their stay might extend to weeks or even months. One immigrant family told that it was sometimes so crowded in their home that one had to walk carefully at night so as not to step on those who were sleeping on the floor. As the immigrants' economic conditions improved, they built bigger and better houses, often converting the first house to a shed or animal shelter.

Most immigrants were unaccustomed to luxury in Norway and found little in America. Home furnishings were simple in design and made of wood. Whether brought from Norway or made in America, stools, benches, tables, beds, shelves, and cupboards were made by hand with simple tools. If time and talent allowed, some pieces were ornately decorated, but for the most part, furniture was entirely utilitarian.

Oxen were used as draft animals for plowing the land and hauling loads to market. A type of wagon commonly used by Norwegian immigrants was the *kubberulle*. Its name was derived from the wheels, which were made from slices of a tree trunk, and the edge of the wheel covered with an iron band to make it more durable. In this crude contraption drawn by a team of oxen, grain was hauled to, or fetched from, the nearest market. Over time, horses replaced oxen, and improved farm implements replaced the old plows, grain cradles, and reapers, which were first used on farms. Eventually, better wagons, as well as buggies, came into common use among rural Norwegians in America.

Though some immigrants arrived at their destination with enough money to buy land, some did not. They usually reached Wisconsin in June or July, often too late to plant a crop, but not too late to cut enough hay to feed a cow during the winter. If they could not purchase land immediately, they found jobs and saved until they had enough to purchase a few acres of land --- something that was unthinkable in Norway. Men could usually find work as hired hands during harvest and the busy season on the farm, cut timber during the winter, or work in the lead mines. During the Civil War, many young men enlisted in the Union army, receiving a bounty in addition to what seemed to them a very high salary. Single ladies went into domestic service in the towns or cities or worked for an immigrant family with many children.

It is said that Norwegian immigrants were tailor-made to develop the vast agricultural resources in the United States, and at this, most were successful. An example is the Norwegian cotter from Hadeland who came to the Koshkonong settlement in 1852. He worked there for a few years before moving to the Vermont settlement in Dane County, Wisconsin, where he purchased 40 acres of land in 1855 for $1.25 per acre. Six years later he bought an additional 40 acres from an American, for which he paid $320 ($8 per acre). Several years later he bought another "40." When the census of 1870 was recorded, this man had $1500 worth of real estate, and $600 worth of personal property, a remarkable estate for a poor *husmann* to accumulate in less than two decades. He was treasurer of the congregation and was involved with church committees and community organizations from the time he first lived in the township, an opportunity he would not have had in Norway. He learned to read and write English, but spoke only Norwegian.

Norwegians often attached descriptive names to people, and this man was no exception. He was known as *Jon ned på veggen* (John down by the road). Immigrants came by train from Milwaukee to Black Earth, and from there they made their way south to the Norwegian settlements. Since John's farm was the first one along the road south of Black Earth which was occupied by a Norwegian, it was there the newly arrived immigrants stopped for food and drink, asked directions to the settlement, and inquired about earlier arrivals.

The Immigrant Church

Religious tradition and expression was deeply ingrained in Norwegians and had a stronger influence on the people than any other aspect of that culture. This significant force was not left behind when the emigrants left Norway but followed them to the immigrant community in the United States.

In Norway, the government built churches and supplied pastors to fill the pulpits, but the organized church, which was taken for granted in the Old Country, did not exist in America. Here the immigrants had to organize their own congregation, call a pastor, and arrange for a teacher to instruct their children in religion. Even those who were not particularly devout were strongly steeped in tradition and felt a compelling need for an ordained minister to administer communion, hold religious services, baptize babies, confirm young people, perform marriages, and conduct burial services.

At first, few pastors were willing to emigrate. They held relatively secure and prestigious positions in Norway, with the assurance of fairly decent incomes. They were reluctant to risk the security of that lifestyle in order to minister to their countrymen in a strange land.

The first clergymen to minister to the Norwegians in America were Elling Eielsen and Claus Lauritz Clausen. Both were ordained in America in October 1843 by German Lutheran clergymen. Eielsen, a Haugen lay preacher with little formal education, represented the low-church point of view. Clausen, a Dane who had moved to Norway, came to America to become a teacher of immigrant children and was coaxed into becoming a pastor for the people at Muskego in Wisconsin. There he built the first Norwegian Lutheran Church in this country.

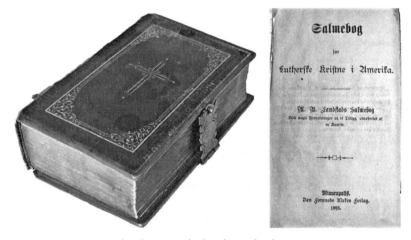

Salmebog (Psalmbook) and title page

Another set of religious attitudes was established among the Norwegian immigrants when Rev. J. W. C. Dietrichson arrived in America. Having been educated at the University of Norway, and ordained there before coming to America, he advanced the highly orthodox form of Lutheranism. He arrived in 1844 to serve the people at Rock Prairie, Jefferson Prairie, and Koshkonong in Wisconsin. During his term, the very formal high-church form of the Norwegian Lutheran Church was established in America. In addition to serving congregations at Koshkonong, Dietrichson traveled to other settlements. He held services in homes, barns, school houses, and sometimes under a shade tree in the summer. One of his trips took him to Springdale Township, Dane County, Wisconsin, in April 1850. A notice in the Norwegian immigrant newspaper announced that Dietrichson would baptize babies brought to him there. People came from all around, and 18 babies were baptized on the appointed day.

Dietrichson returned to Norway in 1850 and was replaced by Rev. A. C. Preus. Preus was instrumental in organizing the Norwegian Synod in America and became its first president. He advised congregations of pastoral candidates in Norway and assisted in directing letters of call to Norwegian clergy. He also visited Norway and helped persuade Norwegian pastors and lay preachers to serve in the United States. Candidates for the ministry who went to America before their ordination were ordained by Rev. Preus when they arrived in Chicago.

Letters of call to Norwegian pastors were for a term of 5 years of service. Not only must they serve the parish to which they were called, but they were also expected to travel to neighboring settlements several times a year. They spent about a week in each area, holding *gudstjeneste* (divine services), *oppbyggelse* (prayer meetings), confirmation services, and performed other ministerial duties while there.

A schedule of services to be held in the Norwegian settlements was published in the Norwegian language and appeared in one of the early Norwegian-American newspapers, *Emigranten* (The Emigrant). Rev. H. A. Preus of Spring Prairie (a cousin of A. C. Preus), announced the following services in August 1855:

North Blue Mounds – Saturday, Sept. 8, 10:00 a.m.
South Blue Mounds & Springdale – Sunday, Sept. 9, 10:00 a.m.
Perry – Tuesday, Sept. 11, 10:00 a.m.
Primrose – Wednesday, Sept. 12, 2:00 p.m.

Immigrant Congregation Rules for Church Order

An example of an immigrant congregation was that in Vermont Township, Dane County, Wisconsin. It was organized according to the order of the church in Norway in 1856. A letter of call was sent to Rev. Brodahl in Norway to come and serve several settlements. A parsonage was built, and soon Rev. Brodahl, his wife, and several children arrived from Norway to serve the parish. The head church was at Perry, and Vermont was an annex congregation without a church. At first, services were held in a schoolhouse in the village, but later the people of the Vermont congregation bought an abandoned school building and moved it to the Norwegian settlement south of town. It was used until a proper church could be built. Worship services were to be held at the head church on Sundays and in the annex churches on weekdays.

Vermont Lutheran Church, Dane County, WI
Built in the 1860s

A *medhjelper* (pastor's assistant) was selected from among the most sincere and God-fearing members of the congregation. It was his responsibility to direct the churchly affairs of the congregation and to aid in establishing proper Christian conduct. Trustees were elected to govern the temporal affairs of the congregation. Each congregation employed a *lærer* (teacher) who was responsible for instructing children in preparation for confirmation and chose a *klokker* (sexton) to lead the singing and read scripture passages. The *klokker* sat near the pastor during the worship service, and led the singing of hymns, sometimes accompanied by a *salmodikan* (a one-stringed instrument played with a bow). He received his salary as part of the offering from the congregation. His portion was laid on a separate table from that where the portion for the pastor was placed. Apparently, his portion was meager as the saying continued to apply in this country as it had in Norway: "When it rains on the pastor, it drips on the *klokker.*" One of the church members was chosen to supply bread and wine for communion, the cost of which was covered by the payment of 5 cents by each communicant.

Rules of conduct during church services were established. These rules stated:

1. No one is allowed to leave during the opening prayer or the Lord's Prayer.

2. No one ought to, unless necessary, go out of the church before the service is finished.

3. Parents with children are reminded that silence should be maintained during the service, as far as possible.

4. The elected, dedicated men honor these rules and carry them out as far as possible.

Later, rules were laid down regarding non-members who participated in congregational activities without giving financial support to the church. In order to have a child baptized in the congregation, a non-paying family was to pay the congregation $5, the pastor $1, and the sexton or cantor (*klokker* or *kirkesanger*) 50 cents.

The pastor was responsible for conducting the business of the congregation with the help of the most capable men in the congregation. It was his responsibility to record all ministerial acts which he performed. Until permanent congregations were established, ministerial acts were recorded in the records of the pastor's head church.

A committee was elected by an association of pastor's assistants and trustees to determine the pastor's salary for the congregation. When a church was built each farmer was assessed in proportion to his or her assets and circumstances. One committee was elected to investigate the purchase of building materials and another to assess funds for building a church. Regular church dues averaged about $4.50 per member per year in the 1860s, and an additional $8 to $10 was assessed annually when the church was built. At a time when a man's wages were 50 cents per day, his contribution to the church was his total wages from several weeks' work.

Church Controversy in the 1860s

Religious conflict existed in the Norwegian immigrant community from the beginning, the result of which was the formation of several Lutheran synods in America. Conflict was not created by the immigrants, but by the inclination on the part of Norwegian clergy to perpetuate the great social chasm that existed between themselves and the immigrants. The immigrants had crossed an ocean to be "free," only to find that class stratification had followed them to America. Furthermore, it is doubtful that Norwegian emigrants were deeply concerned about the technical aspects of theology and ecclesiasticism. Their main religious concern was to have an ordained Norwegian minister to administer sacraments of the church, conduct worship services, and aid them in practicing their religion as they believed was fitting and proper.

About 55,000 Norwegians had immigrated by 1860. At that time there were nearly 100 Norwegian Lutheran clergymen. According to some authorities, fewer than 50 formally educated Norwegians lived in the United States before 1860, most of them being ministers. Other educated Norwegians in this country at that time were teachers or the spouses of ministers.

Between 1860 and 1870, 65,000 people left Norway, most of them coming to America. This resulted in the organization of additional congregations. Pastors from Norway were called to serve churches in the immigrant community and remained in America. However, many others returned to Norway when their term of service was over.

Church organization did not always go smoothly in the immigrant communities. The decade of the 1860s was an especially difficult time. Conflict brewed over lay preaching versus strict orthodoxy, public school versus parochial school, and the issue of slavery received national attention. Many leaders of the Norwegian Synod did not believe that slavery in and of itself was contrary to Biblical teachings, although most immigrants believed that it was.

The form of Lutheranism accepted by some immigrants was that of the Haugeaners. They did not approve of drinking, dancing, card-playing, theater, and some secular literature. Their pastors often came from the rural class of people in Norway and were not of the intellectual elite, as were most of the clergymen of the Norwegian synod. Some Norwegians favored the highly orthodox church, with its formal liturgical service, and others preferred advanced religious practices that did not fit either group. The result was the organization of several Synods to accommodate the divergent religious views of the immigrants.

Funeral Customs in the Immigrant Community

Mortuaries and funeral directors were unknown to the early settlers. The responsibility for preparing the body of the deceased and providing a coffin rested with the family. A coffin of ordinary lumber was constructed and painted black with *kjønrøk* (lampblack). Looped pieces of rope formed handles along the sides of the coffin. The inside was lined with white muslin, and a muslin shroud was made for the body. An ordinary farm wagon or sled served as a hearse.

Most often the deceased was buried by the family. If death was due to a highly contagious disease, burial took place immediately to reduce the danger of exposure to the disease. Under ordinary circumstances, the family and friends gathered for the burial and read appropriate Scripture passages. They sang hymns such as *"Lov og takk og evig ære"* (Praise and thanks and eternal glory), or "Når liv og ånd" (When our life and spirit depart). That custom from the Old Country continued to be a part of the burial service for many years in America.

Until a church was built, the cemetery was in a pasture or on a hillside on the Urness farm. Tombstones, as we know them, were rarely used except in the case of a very prominent person. Grave markers of wood, containing the name of the deceased and perhaps an appropriate inscription, were commonly used. A favorite in the Vermont Lutheran cemetery was "*Salig er den døde, some døde I Herren*" (Blessed are the dead who die in the Lord).

Immigrant Monument side A

Immigrant Monument side B

In early church records, it is noted that the date of death and the date of the committal service were sometimes several weeks or months apart. This was a common practice in Norway also. When it was very cold in winter, the ground was solidly frozen, it was necessary to delay the burial until a grave could be dug. The minister would conduct the committal service the next time he was in the area. In later years, when the parish had its own minister and it was easier for the minister to travel about in his parish, funerals and committal services were held soon after a death occurred. Even then, the body was prepared at home and placed in the homemade coffin. The minister came to the home, where a short service was conducted, before taking the coffin to the church for a formal funeral service, and burial in the church cemetery. After photographers were established in the immigrant community, the deceased was often photographed in the coffin.

Education of Norwegian Immigrant Children

Children in rural Norway attended ambulatory schools, where they received instruction for confirmation in the Norwegian State Church. A school law was passed in Norway in 1848, establishing schools in the towns, but ambulatory schools were considered adequate for the education of peasant children. Thus, the tradition of holding school in the home was continued in the Norwegian immigrant community during the early years of the American settlements.

The compulsory school law was not passed in Wisconsin until 1879, so until that time Norwegian immigrants had the choice of sending their children to common school, to Norwegian school, or to no school at all. Norwegian school was an *omgangsskole* (traveling school) and moved from one house to another, remaining as many days in each house as the owner was willing to fund. The teacher was always a man; the early Norwegian clergy had little faith in the teaching abilities of women. They were very critical of the common school in America and consider women teachers to be inept. The earliest teachers of immigrant children were trained in Norway, perhaps at Latin School, or had served as ministers' assistants before coming to America.

Subjects taught in the immigrant traveling school included catechism and its explanation, Bible history, hymn study, writing, and arithmetic. All pupils participated in the religious subjects, but only the older ones were taught to write and cipher. It was necessary to read in order to be confirmed, but writing was not considered important, particularly for girls. Pupils were rated on singing ability, intellect, conduct, effort, and accomplishment.

A *skolesubscription* list was prepared by the school committee of the congregation, and each farmer was expected to contribute the amount of money that would pay the teacher's salary for 1 to 4 days.

Grandpa's Primer

The man appointed to collect these funds was called the *skole tilsynsmand*. After the area was divided into public school districts, a man was appointed to collect funds in each district. In 1862, teachers received 40 to 50 cents per day.

As early as 1863, the Vermont Lutheran congregation decided to have three to four months of religious school. Children of non-paying families were not to be deprived of a religious education but were allowed the privilege of attending parochial school. In 1869, it was decided to hold eight months of Norwegian school the coming year, one month consisting of twenty-six days, of which two days were for examinations. Some teachers complained about teaching in homes, as it was not conducive to learning. After public schools were built, religious school moved out of the homes. The public schoolhouse was used for Norwegian School when common (elementary) school was not in session.

During the time of conflict over religious versus public school, controversy raged in the Norwegian settlements. It was a favorite topic to be expounded upon in the Norwegian-American press and resulted in irreversible schisms in many congregations. Most Norwegian settlers did not oppose free public school, but were not ready to give up religious school when the public school was not in session.

The first books used in Norwegian School were: Lokensgaard's ABC Bog, Luther's Catechism, Pontoppidan's Explanation, Bible History, a reading book, and the hymn book, all in the Norwegian language. Children were required to memorize Luther's Catechism, the Explanation, Bible passages, and many hymns. Early religious schools taught not only religion to the Norwegian immigrants and their descendants but helped to preserve their culture and heritage. Well into the 20th century, the Norwegian School curriculum in the settlements contained stories and poems depicting Norway's heroes, writers, and artists, accounts of Norwegian settlements in the United States, and other subjects about Norway and Norwegians. Perhaps "Norwegian School" was a more appropriate name than "Religious School," as "Norwegianness" was taught as well as religious subjects. Not only did it provide a solid Christian background, but helped to perpetuate the Norwegian heritage. Eventually, as English became a part of their daily lives, it was integrated into the classroom as well.

Rovang School - parochial school built in 1880 in rural Decorah
Vesterheim Norwegian-American Museum, Decorah, IA

The Norwegian Immigrant Press

The immigrant press played an important role in the Norwegian-American community of the United States and provides a glimpse of conditions in the settlements of the mid-1800s. In addition to the usual newspaper articles, the immigrant press became an instrument through which controversial subjects such as religion, education, and language could be discussed and debated among the immigrants.

The first Norwegian language newspaper published in America, *Nordlyset,* appeared in 1847 and was followed by others, among them, *Emigranten,* which was printed near Orfordville, Wisconsin, and later in Madison. *Emigranten,* dated January 30, 1852, defined its purpose in an article, "To Our American Friends." It states, in part:

> *"...the true interest of our people in this country is to become Americanized as soon as possible and be one with the Americans. In this way alone can they fulfill their destiny and contribute their part to the final development of the character of this great nation."*

Emigranten
Vesterheim Norwegian-American Museum, Decorah, IA

Issues of *Emigranten* in 1854 and 1855 contained articles of information about events taking place in the nation and in the world. Other articles were aimed directly at helping newly arrived immigrants make the transition from Norwegian citizens to American citizens. Among advertised items were tools, furniture, groceries, pills, eyeglasses, daguerreotype portraits, tobacco, religious books, bookbinders – all goods and services available to the immigrants in the United States.

The newspaper also contained inquiries to assist people in locating friends or relatives who had arrived in this country or moved away without leaving a forwarding address. Some people were sought because they owed someone money. A half-grown boy was looking for work as a herd boy. A ship company advertised opportunities for immigrants to visit the land of their birth, or to send packages or money to Norway. Daily and weekly American newspapers, printed in New York and Milwaukee, were advertised. Strayed animals were sought and churches and schools announced vacancies for qualified teachers and pastor's assistants. In 1854, an announcement was made of the opening of the railroad line from Canada through Niagara Falls, Hamilton, Detroit, Chicago, Galena, to St. Louis, and all points west — a total of 1,200 miles.

The scope of readership far exceeded the number of subscriptions. Newspapers were passed from one family to another, and information was passed by word of mouth to others. In this manner, news became widely dispersed throughout the settlement.

Skandinaven was founded in 1866 as a weekly publication in Chicago. After the Great Chicago Fire in 1871, they began publishing a daily newspaper. The last issue of *Skandinaven* was October 31, 1941.

Skandinaven
Vesterheim Norwegian-American Museum, Decorah, IA

Decorah-Posten og Ved Arnen was a notable Norwegian language newspaper founded in 1874 by Brynild Anundsen, who came from Skien, Norway. It was distributed weekly via mail and widely read by the Norwegian community. One of my father's favorites was the comic strip *Han Ola og Han Per* created by Peter Rosendahl. The newspaper was in circulation for 99 years. Anundsen Publishing, in business since 1868, is still thriving in Decorah and is the publisher of this book.

Decorah Posten
Vesterheim Norwegian-American Museum, Decorah, IA

Norwegians were eager to become Americans and adopt the ways of America in business and politics, yet they were reluctant to discard the mother tongue, and customs from the Old Country, in their churches and homes. Evidence of this strong ethnic heritage lingers in the nature of many Norwegian-Americans into the 21st century.

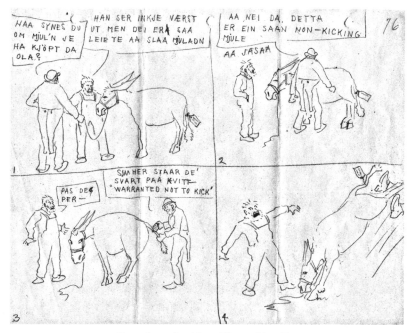

Drawings for *Han Ola og Han Per*
Vesterheim Norwegian-American Museum, Decorah, IA

Translation:

1. Per: What do you think of the mule I bought, Ola?
   Ola: He doesn't look so bad.

2. Per: Oh, no then. That's a genuine "non-kicking" mule.
   Ola: Watch out Per!

3. Per: It says right here in black and white, "Warranteed not to kick."

4. Uff-da!

Chapter 12

NORWEGIAN NAMING TRADITIONS

N aming traditions used in Norway in the 19th century and before, are unique to that country. Each person was identified
by three names: The given or Christian name, the patronym, and the farm name. Understanding the system is of great help
when trying to locate one's Norwegian ancestors.

The Given Name

The given name, or Christian name, was not chosen by the parents
of the child in the same manner as we choose names today. An established pattern dictated what each successive child born in a given
family would be named, and it was a general rule that the child was
baptized by that name by the time he or she was eight days old, or as
soon as the pastor was available to perform the rite.

The first son was almost always named for the father's father, the
first daughter for the father's mother, the second son for the mother's
father, and the second daughter for the mother's mother. There were
exceptions to this rule. If the couple took over the mother's home
farm, the firstborn child might be given the name of the maternal
grandparent, and the second child of the same sex received the name
of the paternal grandparent. Successive children were named after
deceased siblings, deceased aunts, uncles, great grandparents, etc.

An unusual custom was practiced in naming children born
to those who remarried following the death of a spouse. The first
daughter born to a man by his second wife was given the name of
the man's deceased wife, and the first son born to a woman by her
second husband was given the name of her deceased husband.

Rarely was a son named for his father, as is the case with "junior" as we know it today; however, a son could have the same name as his father in cases where the grandfather's and father's names were the same. Another situation where a son might have the name of the father was when the boy's father died before his birth. In this instance, it was common to name the child for the deceased father.

It is not unusual to find two children in a family having the same given name. In a family where the father's father was named Ole, and the mother's father was also named Ole, the couple was obliged to name a son for each of the grandfathers. When two full brothers had the same name, a distinction was made by adding *d.e.* or *d.y.* after the name, indicating *den eldre* (the elder), or *den yngre* (the younger).

The two most common names used in Norway, before the turn of the century, were Ole and Anna. They were used throughout most of Norway, but some given names were unique to certain districts. An example of this is the name Thomas, which is most often found in Årdal in Sogn.

The vast majority of Norwegians were of the rural class of people, who traditionally gave their children only one Christian name. It was only in the city and among the upper-class families that it was common to give children more than one name at baptism. A child born to a servant couple in Bergen, in 1834, received two given names when she was baptized at the Cathedral there. Soon after she was baptized, the parents and baby moved back to their home district of Sogndal, where they lived on a farm. The four children born to the family in Sogndal received only one Christian name, as was customary among rural folks. Perhaps it was their status as city-dwellers at the time that motivated them to give their first-born child two names.

Naming children according to the established pattern continued among the Norwegians after they immigrated to the United States. Eventually, the system was modified to allow for more American-sounding names, and even substituting the American equivalent for Norwegian names; but it was still important that the name began with the same initial or sound as the grandparent's name. This way, the name would sound less old-fashioned than the Norwegian name, yet the grandparent was honored, and the old system preserved.

The Patronym

The patronym was the second name by which a Norwegian was identified. It was the name of the father plus the "son" ending (usually spelled "sen") to identify men and boys; the father's name plus "datter" was used to identify women and girls. The spelling of the male patronym often causes comment. Should it be "sen" or "son?" It doesn't matter. The Danish form is "sen," the Swedish form is "son" or "sson." For over four centuries before 1814, Norway was ruled by Denmark, the country where most Norwegian officials and clergy received their education; therefore, we can expect to see the Danish form of spelling used in the records of Norway. In America, Norwegians often adopted the "son" ending, simply because that was how the word for a father's male offspring was spelled in this country.

The patronym was a permanent name. It did not change when a girl married. There was not a maiden name in the Norwegian naming system. A girl was always her father's daughter, even after marriage, so she continued to be identified by the same patronym. The church records of Norway, as well as those of the immigrant church in this country, show a child of "Ole Pedersen and Anna Larsdatter" being baptized, not a child of "Mr. and Mrs. Ole Pedersen." Even today, Norwegians do not identify themselves as "Mr. and Mrs. Whoever."

The Farm Name

The farm name is the third name by which the Norwegian was identified. Since about 1700 Norway has maintained a list of place names, dwelling places, farms, and holdings. This is called a public estate valuation register. Included in it are names of about 50,000 farms. In addition, many separate holdings or *bruks* are named. In some cases, as many as 100 additional names are found on a single farm. These additional names identify *seters*, forest plots, meadows, hills, coves, lakes, brooks, etc. Some farm names were established so early that they are said to have been the same since prehistoric times. We have known that names of many farms were listed in documents from the

Middle Ages (500-1450), that period between ancient and modern times.

One reason for the farm structure, as well as the naming system, to remain the same for so long is that Norway was never conquered by a foreign power that introduced new systems. The population was not uprooted or disrupted. In other parts of Europe, countries were often the object of political or military conflict, and when not the direct object of conflict, they were often caught in the crossfire. Thus, Norway was able to preserve farm names that were established very early. The name belonged permanently to the farm, being used as the third identifying name by people while they lived at that place. Should they move to another farm, they would no longer use the name of the previous farm but would use the name of the new residence for their third identifying name.

With the increase in population and the fragmentation of farms in Norway, newer farm names came into common usage. Most of these names described the farm's location. Examples are: *Dybdahl*, which means deep valley; *Haug* means hill; *Vik* means inlet, etc. Fewer names describe the occupation of the person living at the farm. An example of such a name is Gesme (*Gjesme* in Norway). It is told that the original spelling was *Giersmed*, meaning spear smith or metal smith.

The farm in Norway did not generally consist of only one household, with the father, mother, and a few children as the only residents. It was more likely made up of several households -- the freeholder, some renters, some cotters, servants, day laborers, and perhaps some pensioned people. Sometimes members of the various households were related by blood, sometimes they were not; yet, everyone living at a given farm used the farm name as part of his or her identifying name. Those who were not landowners often identified themselves by the name of the farm with the ending *eie*, which means "under the ownership of." An example of this is a family of cotters at Eidsand in Hadeland. They used *Eidsandeie* as their farm name. Another means of identification was used by a cotter's family living at the little place, Hagen, on the Kinsedal farm in Sogn. They used "Hagen under Kinsedal" as their farm name. The Norwegian farm name told where the person lived and was little more than an address — be it for the farm owner, or for anyone living there at a given time.

What Happened to the Naming System When Norwegians Immigrated?

The use of surnames was unknown to the immigrant. In addition to being faced with learning a new language when they arrived in America, Norwegian immigrants had to adopt a new naming system. At first, many immigrants used their male patronym (Hanson, Olson, Peterson, Larson, Johnson, etc.) as a surname but after they had been in America for a while they began using the farm name again, this time as a surname. Often modifications in the spelling and pronunciation were necessary to make Norwegian names comprehensible by Americans. Among adaptations were: Braka became Brager; Johannessen became Johnson; Djupedal became Dybdahl; Gjesme became Gesme, etc. Among given names, Jens became James; Lars became Lewis; Brita became Bertha; Unni became June; Guri became Julia, Johannes became John; Kari became Caroline, etc.

It is often said, "When my grandfather came to America, he changed his name..." Seldom did Norwegians truly change their names or take a completely disparate name. They simply decided whether to use the farm name or the patronym and then Americanize it so their Yankee neighbors could handle it.

Recent Naming Practices in Norway

With the adoption of the Naming Law in Norway in 1923, each family was required to have a surname. For the first time surnames were used for everyone. People were told to use either their current patronym or the name of the farm where they were then residing or had been living, which identified them with the rest of their family. Family names have continued since then, down the male line, until 1979, when Norway passed a Personal Names Act. This provides for choosing a family name. A couple can use either the husband's or the wife's family name — or each can keep the name they had before marriage. A child born to this couple must be given either of the family names of the parents by the time the child is six months old. If by that time the parents have not notified authorities of the child's family name, the child will receive the family name of the mother. These rules apply both to children born in wedlock and those born out of wedlock. Before a baby is baptized, the given name must be approved, as some names are not permitted.

According to *Norway Times/Nordisk Tidende*, May 16, 1985, the rules for changing one's name in Norway were eased in 1984, and as a result, 27,000 Norwegians dropped their old names. Some surnames are protected, but in general, it is not difficult to change your name in Norway today. You simply have to report the fact to the national register. Think of the confusion this will create for genealogists!

Spelling Inconsistencies

Norwegian names have a broad variety of spellings, none of which are actually <u>wrong</u>. This is explained by the fact that there were no spelling rules in Norway until after 1900. Names were spelled as they sounded to the person making the entry in the church or government record. In the early 1800s, that person was usually someone who had been educated in Denmark and used the Danish form of spelling. In early times it was not unusual to find poorly trained clergymen and officials serving churches in Norway's remote country districts. Their lack of training helped little in establishing a standard form for spelling names. At a time when the common people did not write or read handwriting, there was no one to object to the form of spelling an official used when recording a person's name.

Spelling inconsistencies continued throughout the period of emigration, well into the 1900s. The names of many Norwegians were completely incomprehensible to the American immigration officials, who had no idea of how to spell Norwegian names. Not least among those guilty of making errors in recording names were the clergymen who came to serve the immigrant church in America. Confused and inept scribes of the past are responsible for recording our ancestors' names, creating untold frustrations for those researching the records today.

SEVEN GENERATION RELATIONSHIP CHART							
Common Progenitor	1 child	2 grand child	3 g g child	4 2 gg child	5 3 gg child	6 4 gg child	7 5 gg child
1 child	sis or bro	niece/ nephew	great n / n	g g n / n	2 g g n / n	3 g g n / n	4 g g n / n
2 grandchild	niece/ nephew	1st cousin	1 cou 1 rem	1 cou 2 rem	1 cou 3 rem	1 cou 4 rem	1 cou 5 rem
3 g g child	grand n / n	1 cou 1 rem	2nd cousins	2 cou 1 rem	2 cou 2 rem	2 cou 3 rem	2 cou 4 rem
4 2 gg child	g g n / n	1 cou 2 rem	2 cou 1 rem	3rd cousins	3 cou 1 rem	3 cou 2 rem	3 cou 3 rem
5 3 gg child	2 g g n / n	1 cou 3 rem	2 cou 2 rem	3 cou 1 rem	4th cousins	4 cou 1 rem	4 cou 2 rem
6 4 gg child	3 g g n / n	1 cou 4 rem	2 cou 3 rem	3 cou 2 rem	4 cou 1 rem	5th cousins	5 cou 1 rem
7 5 gg child	4 g g n / n	1 cou 5 rem	2 cou 4 rem	3 cou 3 rem	4 cou 2 rem	5 cou 1 rem	6th cousins

gg = great grand
n/n = niece/nephew
cou = cousin
rem = removed

To find your relationship with another individual begin with the "common progenitor" in the gray area in the upper left-hand corner of this chart. Read to the right and select your relationship to the common progenitor. Then, again starting in the upper left-hand corner of this chart look down to select the other person's relationship to the "common progenitor." Draw a line down from the person on the horizontal axis and another line left to right from the person on the vertical axis. Where they intersect is your relationship with each other.

GLOSSARY OF
NORWEGIAN WORDS

alen	measurement equal to about 2 ft
bearlage	inviting circle
bedemann	inviting man
beinings	gifts of food
benk	bench
bispedømme	diocese
bord	table
bønder	free-holder or farm-owner
brennevin	brandy
bruk	rental unit operated by tenant
bu	simple storehouse
bunad	festive folk costume
bygdebøker	local Norwegian histories
den elder (d.e.)	the elder
den yngre (d.y.)	the younger
do	privy
dugurd	late forenoon breakfast
eldhus	cook house
fattiglem(mer)	pauper(s) or begger(s)
fekar	drover - dealing with livestock
fjøs	cow barn
flatbrød	flat bread

flyttedager .... moving days - Apr 14 & Oct 14

forbud .... reservations

fot .... measurement equal to 1 ft.

framskap .... cupboard

frokost .... breakfast

fylker .... counties

gammeløst .... old, aged cheese

gard .... farm

gardmann .... free-holder or farm-owner

geitehus .... goat house

goro .... pastry made on a special iron

graut .... mush

gravfest .... burial festival

gravøl .... burial beer

grisehus .... pig house

grøt .... mush

gudstjenester .... divine worship service

herred .... township

høgsete .... high seat

hønsehus .... hen house

hud, huder .... tanned hides and skins

hulder .... wicked woman with a cow tail

huldre folk .... wicked people of folk lore

husmann .... cotter

husmann's plass .... cotter's place

hussmannsfolk .... sharecropper

husmannsstue .... cotter's living room

ildjern .... firesteel

innerst .... resident farm laborer

jakt .... large sloop

kammer .... store room or sleeping room

kapellan .... apprenticed ordained minister

karjol .... cariole

kirkesanger .... minister's assistant

kjenge .... drinking bowl

kjøgemester .... master of ceremonies

kjønrøk .... lamp black

klokker .... sexton

klokkergård .... sexton's farm

kommune .... municipality

kove .... store room or sleeping room

krakk .... stool

kramkar .... peddler

krumkake .... crisp baked item

krone .... Norwegian currency

kvelds .... supper

kvern .... mill

lærer .... teacher

laup .... unit of measure - about 33 lbs.

låve .... hay barn with a threshing floor

lefse .... thin bread-like food

loft .... dry place to store food and supplies

lutefisk .... treated codfish

mæl, mæler .... unit of measure - about ½ bushel

månedsmatbol .... land needed to feed 1 man/1 mo.

medhjelper .... lay person who assisted the pastor *melkeringe* .... milk tub

menighet .... congregation

mil .... equal to 6.2 miles

mor i buret .... most capable woman at the farm

naust .... boat house

nonetid .... meal eaten around 3pm

odelslov,odelsrett .... allodial law

omgangskole .... rotating or ambulatory school

oppbyggelse .... prayer meetings

øre .... Norwegian currency 100/krone

peis .... fireplace

potetkjeller .... potato cellar

potet klub .... potato cakes and dumplings

prest .... pastor

prestegård .... pastor's farm

prestergjeld .... parish

primøst .... brown cheese

primstav .... 2-sided calendar stick

rakauer .... partially fermented fish

redskapsbu .... tool shed

riksdaler............................. Norwegian coin used until 1875

rommegrøt .... cream porridge

salmodikan .... one-stringed instrument

sauehus .... sheep shelter

sel .... mountain hut

seng .... bed

seter hus .... mountain hut

seter .... summer mountain farm

stift	diocese
skilling	Norwegian currency
skinn	tanned hides and skins
skippund	measure of weight - about 350 lbs.
skole tilsynsmand	man collecting funds for teachers
skoleholder	traveling teacher
skolesubscription	farmers' share of teachers' salary
skydskaarl	post boy
skynd deg	hurry up
skyss	posting station
skyss gutt	errand boy
skyss skifter	posting stations
skytje	woodshed
smalefjøs	animal shelter
smie	blacksmith shop
smørbrød	open-faced sandwich
smørøskje	butter box
sogn	parish
sokn	parish
sør	south
specidaler	Norwegian currency
spikekjøtt	dried meat
stabbur	storehouse
stav	stave
stolkjærre	carriage pulled by one horse
strull	pastry made on a special iron
stue	living room
stueklokken	living room clock

sval .... vestibule

tjenestefolk .... farm servants

tomme .... measurement equal to about 1 in.

tørkehus .... drying house

trev .... hay barn with a threshing floor

tun .... open yard or farmyard

våg .... weight equal to about 39.5 lbs.

vedhus .... woodshed

BIBLIOGRAPHY

Anderson, Edward L., *Six Weeks in Norway*. Cincinnati, R. Clarke and Co., 1877.

Blegen, Theodore C., *Norwegian Migration to America*. NAHA, Northfield, MN, 1940.

Boyesen, Hjalar H., *A History of Norway from the Earliest Times*. London and New York, 1900.

Brace, Charles L., *The Norsk Folk*. Charles Scribner, New York, 1857.

Bremer, Fredrika, *The Homes of the New World*. New York, 1953.

Clough, Ethlyn (Editor), *Norwegian Life*. Detroit, 1909.

Conway, Durwent, *Journey Through Norway*. Constable & Co., Edinburgh, and Hurst, Chance & Co., London, 1829.

Drake, Michael, *Population and Society in Norway 1735-1865*. University Press, Cambridge, 1969.

DuChaillu, Paul B., *Land of the Midnight Sun*. 1881.

Elton, Charles, *Norway: the Road and the Fell*. John Henry & James Parker, London & Oxford, 1864.

Flom, George T., *History of Norwegian Immigration to The United States*. Iowa City, Iowa, 1909.

Forester, Thomas, *Norway and its Scenery*. Henry G. Bohn, London. 1853.

Forester, Thomas, *Rambles in Norway*. Longman, Brown, Green & Longman, London, 1855.

Gade, John Allyne, *The Hanseatic Control of Norwegian Commerce During the Middle Ages*. E.J. Brill, Leiden, Holland, 1951.

Gesme, Ann Urness, *Look to the Rock.... The Dybdahl/Anderson Episode*. 1990.

Gesme, Ann Urness, *Look to the Rock.... The Gesme Episode.* 1985.

Gesme, Ann Urness, *Look to the Rock.... The Talle Episode.* 2005.

Gesme, Ann Urness, *Look to the Rock.... The Urness/Barsness Episode.* 1988.

Gjerseth, Knut, *History of the Norwegian People,* 2 vols. New York, 1915.

Hadeland Bygdebok, Vol. IV. Nationaltrykkeriet, Oslo, 1953.

Handlin, Oscar, *Race and Nationality in American Life,* Boston & Toronto, 1957.

Haugen, I., *Norwegian SciTech News, What do the animals in stave church ornamentation signify?,* Published October 4, 2019, https://norwegianscitechnews.com/2019/04/what-do-the-animals-in-stave-church-ornamentation-signify.

Hodne, Fritz, *An Economic History of Norway 1815-1970.* Tapir Trykk, 1975.

Holloway, John George, *A Month in Norway.* London, 1853.

Hubbard WH. *Public Health in Norway 1603-2003.* Med Hist. 2006;50(1):113-117. doi:10.1017/s0025727300009480

Irgens, Lorentz M., *The roots of Norwegian epidemiology - Norwegian epidemiology in the 19th century.* Norsk Epidemiology 2015; 25, (1-2) p. 21-29.

Johnson, Oscar Albert, *Norges Bønder,* Kristiania, 1919.

Laberg, Jon, *Hafslo Bygd or Ætter.* John Griegs Boktrykkeri, Bergen, 1926.

Laing, Samuel, *Journal of a Residence in Norway During the Years 1834, 1935 and 1836.* London, 1937.

Larsen, Karen, *A History of Norway.* Princeton University Press, New York, 1948.

Lovoll, Odd, *The Promise of America.* University of Minnesota Press, Minneapolis, 1984.

Lowe, Emily, *Unprotected Females in Norway.* G. Routledge & Co, London, 1857.

Malthus, T.R., *Essay on the Principle of Population*. London, N.Y., & Melbourne, 1890.

Metcalfe, Frederick, *The Oxonian on the Telemarken*. Volume II, London, 1858.

Narvestad, Carl & Amy, *Valdres Samband 1899-1974*. Granite Falls, MN, 1974.

Nelson, E. Clifford, & Fevold, Eugene L., *The Lutheran Church Among Norwegian Americans*. Vol. I, Augsburg Publishing House, Minneapolis, MN, 1960.

News of Norway, March 27, 1981.

Norges Kultur Historie. *Det Glenfodte Norge*. Bind 4. H. Aschehoug & Co., Oslo, 1980.

Norske Bygder, Bind IV, Sogn. John Griegs Forlag, Bergen, 1937.

Norsk Bygder, Bind V, Sogn. John Griegs Forlag, Bergen, 1937.

Norway, Official Publication for the Paris Exhibition 1900, Kristiania, 1900.

Norway Times/Nordisk Tidende, May 16, 1985.

Norwegian-American Studies and Records Vol. 1-20. NAHA, Northfield, MN, 1926-1959.

Norwegian-American Studies Vol. 21-32. NAHA, Northfield, MN, 1960-1989.

Øverland, Orm, *From America to Norway – Norwegian-American Immigrant Letters 1838 – 1914*, Vol. 1, 1838-1870. NAHA, University of Minnesota Press, 2014.

Pritchett, Robert, Gamle Norge. *Rambles and Scrambles in Norway*. London, 1879.

Public health in Norway 1603-2003. Medical history. 50(1), 113–117. https://doi.org/10.1017/s0025727300009480.

Qualley, Carlton C., *Norwegian Settlements in the United States*. Northfield, MN, 1938.

Rygh, Oluf, *Norske Gaardnavne*, Oslo, 1898-1936.

Scandinavia Past & Present, Arnkrone, Denmark, 1959.

Schmidt, J. L., (2019, August 7), *The Emigranten and Other Norwegian-Language Papers,* retrieved March 4, 2021, from Wisconsin 101 Our History in Objects, *https://wi101.wisc.edu/2019/08/07/norwegian-language-papers.*

Semmingson, Ingrid, (Trans. Einar Haugen), *Norway to America.* University of Minnesota Press, Minneapolis, MN 1978.

Sturluson, Snorre, *Heimskringla, Sagas of the Norse Kings, The Olaf Sagas,* written in Old Norse, app. 1225 A.D.

The Skandinaven, retrieved March 4, 2021, from Chicagology: *https://chicagology.com/newspapers/skandinaven/.*

Tourist Magazine. Western Norway Tourist Magazine, Bergen.

Travelers Discovering Norway in the Last Century, an anthology, Oslo, 1968. Dyersforlag Publisher, E. A. Butgenshon, Editor.

Ulvestad, Martin, *Nordmendene i Amerika, 1907.* Minneapolis, History Companies Forlag.

Ulvestad, Martin, *Nordmenden i Amerika 1913.* Minneapolis, History Companies Forlag.

Valdres Bygdebok, Vol. 5, parts 1 & 2, Gjøvik, 1964.

Valdres Bygdebok, Vol. 6 Leira, Valdres, 1968.